Deyan Sudjic was born in London in 1952, of Yugoslav parents. He was educated at Latymer Upper School and the University of Edinburgh, where he graduated in architecture in 1976. Having qualified, he decided not to practise as an architect, but to write about the subject instead, 'on the grounds both that it was likely to be a more interesting occupation, and that it would spare the world from yet more leaky and mediocre buildings'. He has contributed to *The Times*, *Time Out*, *Design* and *Interiors*, and is now the editor of *Blueprint*. Deyan Sudjic was appointed architecture correspondent of *The Sunday Times* in 1980 and has been a frequent contributor to its pages on subjects such as consumerism, conservation and travel, besides architecture and design.

Paladin Granada Publishing

Deyan Sudjic

Cult Objects

With photographs by Ian Dobbie

The complete guide to having it all

Paladin Books
Granada Publishing Ltd
8 Grafton Street, London W1X 3LA

Published by Paladin Books 1985

Text copyright © Deyan Sudjic 1985

ISBN 0-586-08483-5

Printed and bound in Great Britain

Set in Century Expanded

Original Photography © Ian Dobbie
1985

The publishers would like to thank
all the manufactures and PR
agencies who kindly supplied
photographs for inclusion:

Aga-Rayburn 22; Airstream Inc. 146,
147; American Express 21; Aram
Designs Ltd 101, 102, 107; Artemide
Ltd 69, 103; Austin Rover
Group 126, 127, 139; Autran & Seita
116; Bang & Olufsen UK, Ltd 59;
Barbour & Sons Ltd 86; Bausch &
Lomb 37; Bic Biro UK 40; Bulova
Watch Co. 33; Cartier 12, 13; Citroen
136, 137; Coca Cola GB, Ltd 113;
General Motors Corporation 130;
Gucci 77; Ital Design 141; Jaguar
Cars Ltd 128, 138; Knoll
International 92, 97; Land Rover Ltd
142, 143; E Leitz Instruments Ltd
61, 62; Levi Strauss 80, 81; Raymond
Loewy International Ltd 115;
London Regional Transport 150;
MontBlanc Simplo GmbH 9; Alex
Moulton Ltd 153; Newcastle
Breweries Ltd 120; Olivetti UK 54;
Olympus Optical Co. Ltd 63; Parker
Pens Ltd 41; Polaroid UK, Ltd 64;
Sinclair Research Ltd 14; Thonet
GmbH 95; Uniroyal Ltd 87; VAG
UK, Ltd 134, 135, 144, 145; Volvo
140

and the following for supplying
objects for photography:

Fisher Pen Co. Nevada 43, 44;
Herman Miller 108; The Science
Museum 66, 104; Paul Smith 45

Contents

Chapter One

Are you what you own?

Conspicuous redundancy and the strange phenomenon of a diver's watch. Why real men use Zippos, and when four-wheel drive is the only way to go shopping

Left: Unnecessarily butch though it may be for the everyday needs of the commuter, the Jeep's enduring all-American appeal has kept it looking as desirable as ever for its enthusiasts, and set the pace for the competition

Consider the Jeep for a moment. What is it about an original 1942 specimen restored to mint condition, its drab olive paintwork retouched with a reverence normally reserved for flaking Rembrandts, steel foot pedals worn smooth with age, and enough equipment lashed to the sides to dig it out of a shell crater, that makes otherwise perfectly sensible graphic designers go weak at the knees and use it on suburban shopping trips? There are more practical, and more economical, ways of intimidating the average hatchback driver into the slow lane, too. The four-wheel drive surefootedness of the Jeep and its progeny is spectacularly redundant for the everyday needs of people in artificially aged leather flying jackets and lurid green spectacles. And yet, without even a hard top, their expensive Hasselblads and miniature car stereos are permanently at risk from light-fingered passersby.

Driving a Jeep in town is a bit like buying baked beans in the food hall at Fortnums, or boiling an egg on a restaurant griddle. Rationally speaking, there is no call for all that excess potential. Yet there is something curiously comforting about it, something that marks the Jeep out, as being not just *any* car, but something special.

In much the same way, the glossy black Mont Blanc Diplomat, a fountain pen as fat and as heavy as a torch, may be just the thing to dash off a peace treaty, but it seems a little excessive for a shopping list. It contrives, however, to be effortlessly superior to lesser breeds of writing implement. A felt-tip pen can be persuaded to slip across fine textured writing paper just as satisfyingly smoothly. And a 24-carat gold barrel will drop much more unambiguous hints about numbered Swiss bank accounts, social aspirations and a Bentley in the garage. But neither will have quite the same comfortingly balanced feel when deployed ready for action in the palm, nor do they have that little snow-peak white crown.

Brandish a Mont Blanc, and people will know that it is expensive. Yet it also carries, in coded but unmistakable terms, the message that this is no mere ostentatious status symbol. It is authoritative without having to raise its voice: it is the carefully selected possession of an individual of taste and distinction, one who is serious about getting the best, but who is aware that cost and quality do not necessarily go together. Showing people who understand the code a Mont Blanc is enough to set them off on a whole train of contingent deductions. Own one of those pens, goes the assumption, and you will also own this, wear that, live there and so on. In fact, the Mont Blanc's elaborately archaic air is largely spurious. It is an upstart pretender, a fountain pen born of the Biro and Pentel era, and manufactured in Hamburg by a subsidiary of the Dunhill tobacco empire.

In moments of stress it is just as likely to drip ink over your fingers as any other make, yet even those who have had suits ruined by this propensity remain loyal. They find themselves making allowances, seduced by those buxom and highly polished curves. The reassuring feel of that comforting bulge in the jacket pocket, or in extreme cases, in the V-neck of the Fair Isle has become part of their identity. Heavens, you can't discard all that just because of a leak or two.

Just why the appearance of an anorak anywhere but in the immediate vicinity of large quantities of snow should instantly raise hackles, when an oily looking Barbour – the Solway Zipper, to give it its full name – oozing brute integrity from its brown corduroy collar to its tartan lining is at home anywhere, is one of those great mysteries of the age that repay closer examination. Can you, for example, imagine a Barbour being turned away from Claridges? Scarcely. But nor is it the kind of garment which is likely to inflame passions in the public bar either. Equally a Jeep can confidently be parked in locations in which a Datsun would seem absurdly humble.

Clearly, there are forces at work here which run deeper than mere questions of fashion, status, or even sheer eccentricity, though all of them are involved. There is something about the honest-to-goodness, sturdy but simple lines of the Jeep that embodies in every nut, bolt, dial, gauge and switch that peculiarly American brand of gum-chewing nonchalance about machinery. As indeed it should be. One Karl Probst dashed off the design in a single weekend, presumably locked in the den with a catalogue of standard auto parts, an endless supply of Lucky Strikes, and a wet towel wrapped around his forehead. The U.S. Army invited both the engineering company Willys and Ford to compete for the contract, and to come up with alternative designs for a military vehicle. Probst's design won, and went into production with both firms. The

Jeep, aka the general purpose utility vehicle, may have been built in its millions, but each one of those machines shares an instantly recognizable personality that has the power to turn heads wherever it goes. The Jeep is a character in fact, in a way that the Morris Marinas or Honda Civics of this world will never be.

One theory for the name is that it comes from a strip cartoon hero of the 1930s, who was capable of doing anything, and it could, if true, have something to do with the affection that the Jeep inspired early on in its life. After the war, General Eisenhower even went so far as to credit the Jeep, along with the rather less appealing DC-3, the bazooka and the atom bomb, as one of the four most important war winning weapons that the Allies possessed.

Those martial origins have not prevented the Jeep, like the Citroën 2CV, the Beetle, the Cadillac Eldorado, the Mini, and even the bulbous Morris Minor from coming to symbolize qualities that are recognizable not just to their drivers, who can bask in the reflected glory, but to everybody. They are vehicles whose shapes have worked their way deep into the collective unconscious, celebrated in film, advertising and literature. They have roots and breeding: they are not simply pieces of inanimate metal. The Mont Blanc shares many of these properties. Its flowing curves and baroque flourishes are the very embodiment of the fountain pen. If ever there was a way in

which a pen should look, this is it. And that is a fact of life of which every advertising photographer and art director who has ever used a Mont Blanc as a prop is well aware.

And the Barbour. Made from specially woven twice waxed Egyptian cotton, with dull brass popper studs that fasten with a perceptible and deeply satisfying click that is helped by its patent ball and socket fixing device, and originally designed for grouse moor use, it now speaks quietly but effectively of quality and no-nonsense professionalism. It has the right stuff about it, occupying an aristocratic position at the top of the product family. Holland and Holland make *the* shotgun. Bang and Olufsen make *the* turntable. The Barbour is *the* jacket, even if its makers don't possess a double-barrelled name. Naturally, aristocrats have to conduct themselves with a certain restraint. If they peddle their names too conspicuously, then they devalue them. It would be no good Barbour going into the monogrammed pullovers business if they want to keep their credibility. They would simply go the way of Levi Strauss. The original 501 straight-leg jeans still have conviction, but the company is now hopelessly compromised by countless Levis T-shirts, Levis polyester leisure suits and all the rest of the grisly evidence of milking a good name to death.

The short answer to the question of the Jeep's enduring and curious appeal is that it is, like the Barbour and the Mont Blanc, a

Below: Fat as a torch, the top of the range Mont Blanc Meisterstuck Diplomat is more a 'writing instrument,' as they call it, than a mere fountain pen. But for all its Teutonic style, the pen is now made by a subsidiary of a British tobacco company

10

cult object. It belongs to a class of artefact which exercises a powerful, but mysterious fascination. By definition a cult depends on a group of insiders, tightly knit and linked by secret signs recognizable only to initiates. There is an element of all this to the Jeep, the Mont Blanc and the rest. They have acquired their special status by degrees, initially appealing to small groups of aficionados.

To that curious band of militaria buffs who spend their weekends in motley second-hand uniforms, polishing pet half-tracks and swapping anecdotes about the stitching on standard issue NATO canvas webbing, a Jeep will have a special significance way beyond the comprehension of most of us. It offers, for those who have a mind to, endless possibilities for debating the relative merits of the original Jeep, the sleeker, modern CJ7, or the licence-built Hotchkiss version. A whole cosmology can be constructed on the varying interpretations of the fold-down front window.

But the Jeep is more than that. It is such a potent symbol that it has acquired cult status among a much wider audience than the arcane and slightly dotty confines of the enthusiasts. And the Jeep's glamour has spread. Its concept has been borrowed by other vehicles, from miniature Japanese Range Rover look-alikes to crude Eastern European boneshakers named after appropriately primitive livestock. All of them aspire to the glamour of the Jeep by opting for matt black windscreen wipers or putting wire mesh over the headlamps.

Other cult objects have exerted an immediate mass appeal. There are many cigarette lighters, for example, but there will only ever be one Zippo. With its burnished steel case, fliptop cover and rolling flint, it is an essential prop for countless would-be James Deans. It was originally created in 1932 by George Blaisdell, who seems to have derived his inspiration from the Austrian army, and quickly went on to make a fortune from his instant classic. You don't have to be a smoker, and legend has it that Blaisdell wasn't, to appreciate the sculptural qualities of its shape, or the tactile attractions of that thumb-operated flint. The simple undecorated case is essentially modern, managing at the same time to suggest the slick easy charm of Rick's Café.

Little of this is likely to have been in the mind of Mr Blaisdell at the time. It was, if anything, an unselfconscious piece of design, much in the same way as the Jeep. Utility and cheapness came first, and yet somehow, magic was worked. Instead of looking like an awkward mess of expediency, the components fitted together in both cases in a way that seems all of a piece. Some cult objects, on the other hand, have been designed in the most calculating, deliberate way, setting out to tempt the customer with a stronger lure than simple utility.

Cartier are very keen to tell you that the

firm's founder, Louis Cartier, produced the world's very first purpose manufactured wristwatch in 1904. Cartier made it for his Brazilian airship pilot friend, Alberto Santos-Dumont, to overcome the distracting problem of fumbling for a pocket watch at critical airborne moments. What they are rather more cautious in admitting is that the Santos watch, which they have been marketing since 1978, has little or nothing in common with that early model. Santos-Dumont went up wearing a small round watch secured to his wrist with a supple leather strap. The Santos cleverly draws on the legend, and has been designed to look as if it is a neat and elegant piece of turn-of-the-century proto high tech, with its steel strap and decorative gold screws, but it is really nothing of the kind, being an entirely modern creation. That is not to say it hasn't been an extraordinary success. It is manufactured in hundreds of thousands, and has been the victim of a determined counterfeiting attack, with cheap copies bearing the Cartier name, the characteristic roman numerals and those blue-black sword-shaped hands turning up everywhere from Hong Kong to Berlin. Cartier have fought back with vigour, on one occasion going so far as to hire a steam roller to crush 3000 fake Santos into a metallic pulp. The Santos is a cult object of sorts, but it is too clever for its own good.

The genuine Cartier cult object is the Tank watch, first produced in 1917, and a

Right: For sheer authenticity,
the Tank watch, also by Cartier,
is a much better bet. With its
instrument panel looks, it is an
early example of utilitarian
jewellery

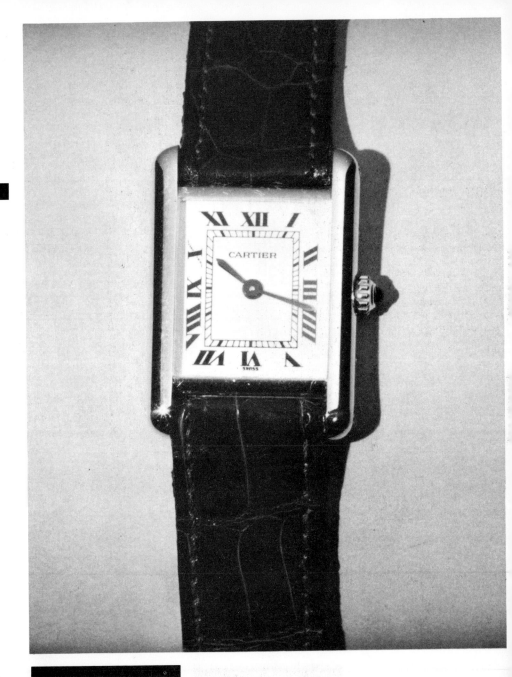

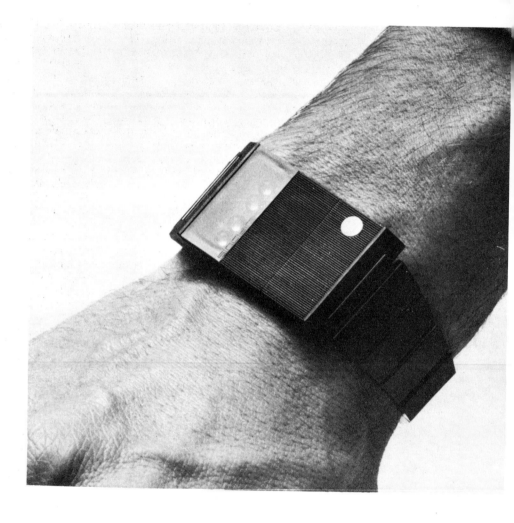

fascinating example of utilitarian instrument gauge looks used for a luxury product. The Tank, along with the early Rolex, rather than the Santos, has the strongest claim to be the earliest wristwatch, designed to be worn on the hand from scratch, and not adapted from the fob and chain. As such it has set the standard by which every watch that has followed should be judged. Yet it was entirely innocent of the calculating artfulness that attended the rebirth of the Santos, and even more so, of the Porsche wristwatch.

Decades after the Tank, the German family that gave the world the Beetle, lent its name, unwillingly in some cases, to a watch that glamorized Teutonic engineering efficiency in so seductive a way that it has had consumers with the price of a secondhand car to spare drooling ever since. By this time, design was out of its adolescent innocence. The Porsche watch took itself as seriously as a Bauhaus building. 'I am a high-minded attempt to design a watch from first principles', is the none too subtle message of its matt black finish and stark geometric shapes. It is, of course, nothing of the kind. The Porsche is a highly sophisticated example of a design that calculatingly adopts the visual language of engineering to give a serious 'professional' look to what is in fact a piece of (price apart) frivolous jewellery. Not surprisingly, the car firm is none too pleased at what they see as an attempt to cash in on their reputation. For all its artfulness, the Porsche watch works. It was designed to be an instant cult object, and it succeeded.

Early in his career, Sir Clive Sinclair almost pulled off the same trick. His Black Watch was the first cheap digital watch ever made, and, in its own way, as pioneering as the first Cartier. Back in 1975 when digitals were such an expensive novelty that they came in cases made from chunks of hollowed-out asteroid, and people wore them on the outside of their jackets for show, Sinclair undercut the whole approach. His version cost less than £20, and looked like the kind of thing you might find nestling in a packet of cornflakes. He didn't just do without the hands, he got rid of the watch face too, leaving only a couple of ribbed rectangular keys, flush with the strap. You pressed one, and the other lit up in red. Everything else was made of grainy black plastic with the texture of rhino hide. Apart from the rather conspicuous business of rolling back your sleeve and pressing buttons when you wanted to tell the time, it was discreet. And it was definitely a 'must-have' product. The trouble was that it didn't work. The cost of replacing faulty microchips nearly sank Sinclair.

Functional difficulties aren't always enough to destroy a product's cult status, but this was going too far. Witness on the other hand the eagerness with which enthusiasts seize upon those Braun toasters that look like Danish town halls of the primly

Left: Clive Sinclair's Black Watch turned digital timekeeping from an overly precious status symbol into a cheap and cheerful piece of matt black with the aesthetics of a cornflake packet give-away. If only the microchips had been as reliable as the design was seductive, Sir Clive would have had a winner. As it was, the Japanese triumphed

elegant variety. They come with instructions in eight languages that adopt – in English at least – the hectoring tone of a drill sergeant to tell you how to make toast. They bark out the precise dimensions in which you should slice your bread. But even if you obey, you will have to resort to pliers to get the toast out more often than not.

These are consciously created cult objects, unlike anonymous and artlessly sophisticated objects such as the Zippo that have no star designer's name attached to them, and no slick advertising campaigns to build their image. That doesn't make them any less powerful or effective at manipulating the consumer. But if the manipulation is to work, it must be done with a sure touch; the moment it falters, the spell is broken. Those dismal props for insecure egos, jeans with a signature scrawled across the back pocket, for example, polo shirts with diminutive reptiles attached to the breast, and pieces of luggage embellished with initials that do not belong to their owners, are all would-be cult objects, and as such all are failures. They try too hard and it shows.

In the nature of things, a cult object has to be mass produced, or at least has to suggest in its shape and finish that it is produced by a machine even if it isn't. It depends for its power on avoiding any impression that it is a one-off, that it is the product of a fallible human hand. It must give the impression at least of the *existence* of limitless numbers of identical copies, hinting at an ideal universal form that is independent of its creator. The feelings that a cult object can promote, however, have much in common with those engendered by certain traditional craft objects. They represent mass production with a human face, machines that have a personality, an identity and a quality that marks them out from the herd of banal everyday objects. The cult object offers a variety of diversions. It can provide the purely hedonistic pleasures of matt black, or that special feeling of being in touch with raw power that comes from controlling a machine with a switch that clicks on and off with just that right kind of a click. Or there is the lofty superiority that comes from knowing that you have the *best* racing bicycle, or binoculars, or Wellington boots, or whatever, even if nobody else will ever notice, thanks to the obscurity of the brand name and the reticence of the styling.

Thinking of brand names, note the special pleasure certain types of photographer take in taping over the brand name of their cameras. It is an ambiguous gesture. Are we to assume that they think that carrying around a conspicuous Nikon is too unsubtle a status symbol, or is it that they want to avoid giving trigger-happy militiamen in Beirut even the hint of chrome that might provide a target? Do they want to hint that they have been dodging militiamen, or is it that they can only afford a Praktica? All very tricky.

It is all too easy to assume that machine-made objects, or mass-produced machines, are soulless and remote. In reality, they frequently have the power to inspire enormous affection. Look at the torrid British love affair with the steam engine. A box on wheels powered by electricity or oil does the job of pulling a train far more efficiently, and does away with all that backbreaking toil and grime that is an essential part of the old coal-fired monsters. Yet no British male over the age of thirty is quite free of their spell. There were too many Saturday mornings spent hanging around at the end of station platforms in the 1960s, in short trousers and Aertex shirts, sniffing coal dust and hot steam and watching those dinosaurs clanking by.

The steam engine was a remarkable case of a machine that looked exactly like what it did. It was power personified, all burnished brass pipework and oiled pistons rotating in intricate patterns, clouds of steam escaping from its valve gear, and above all the noise. Ostensibly the product of rational engineering and dispassionate accountancy, the steam engine was in fact one of the most seductive of cult objects, exerting a spell far greater than can be explained by simple utility. The steam engine proves more than adequately that mute machinery is capable of expressing all kinds of messages, both about itself and about its owners and users.

Take such an apparently functional design issue as space hardware. If ever there was an area that one might expect to be devoid of image and styling, this surely would be it. And yet look at the exhibit in Washington's Air and Space Museum that depicts in effigy the Soviet-American space link-up of the early 1970s. Hanging in the entrance hall are the rival superpowers' capsules, caught coupled together *in flagrante delicto*. Here are two craft designed to carry out the same task, and built to the most exacting constraints of weight and materials with no room for excess stylistic baggage. And yet the American craft is clearly a sleek product of Coca-Cola civilization – not surprising when you consider the involvement of Raymond Loewy (the Frenchman who virtually single-handed transformed industrial design into a recognized profession in America) on the fringes of Nasa. It ought to be the neutral embodiment of pure technology, the result of feeding in a set of requirements into an unromantic computer. But next to it is the Russian half of the tableau, which appears to be equipped with Jules Verne's brass portholes, and an antique barber's chair for the comfort of the cosmonaut, and is presumably also the result of the same process. There could be no clearer demonstration of the differences between two cultures.

Neither of these are cult objects in the strict sense, but they do both carry a clear message in their design, which is one of the essential characteristics of the breed. A cult object is not necessarily a fashionable one, but fashion is a variety of cult. Hence the little black dress is a cult object, so is the Hermes scarf, at least of a sort. Levis 501s, unchanged since Mr Strauss perfected the riveted pocket are certainly another, despite the continual erosion of the image of the rest of the Levis range. So are U.S. Air Force pattern leather flying jackets. Though successful cult objects require the visual stamina not to look instantly dated, there are also cults in ephemera. The hula hoop in the 1950s was a cult object in the way that the frisbee was more recently. Or rather, not just any frisbee, but the championship approved Peach, HDX Wham-O 165. The Vespa scooter was a cult object in the 1960s, and there are signs that it is re-emerging as one now. In the late 1960s all kinds of ephemeral consumer items became cults for a while; the paper dress, cardboard furniture, inflatable armchairs. The whole point of them was that they weren't meant to last.

Cost is not a factor in determining what is, and what is not, a cult object. Unless, that is, one is talking about conspicuous consumption cults. And that is to enter the Nieman Marcus world of designer handguns, Beluga Caviar, Dom Perignon, and those rather lurid motor cars built expressly for the purpose of soaking up surplus oil revenues. But this is of course a minority interest, as specialized in its way as train spotting or birdwatching. Mainstream cult objects can be extremely expensive, or cost just a few pence. A Perrier bottle, or a Gauloise packet would both qualify, even when empty.

There are high and low status cults. The former might include green UniRoyal Wellingtons, and the latter the Mark 2 Ford Cortina, equipped with Terry and Rita stickers across the windscreen. These are extremes of course, and they each involve mutually unintelligible vocabularies. If you aren't in the business of spending weekends in the country, then a Wellington boot is just a Wellington boot. Caring about green wellies, or about customized Cortinas are both examples of the practice of using cult objects in a tribal way, for members to identify each other, and to exclude outsiders.

It is in this tribal area, more than in most cults, that national characteristics start to play a part. The British upper classes constantly proclaim their complete indifference to visual sensibilities, professing to despise those who take them seriously. Yet their perceptions are acute enough to spot an excess cuff button, or the deviant lapel stitching that marks out a non-belonger, at a hundred yards.

There are design cults, and kitsch ones too. Spot a metal briefcase on the London underground, and the chances are that it will contain such other quintessential designer cult objects as a Filofax diary-cum-address book, a Braun pocket calculator, a Rotring drawing pen, and that their owner will be clad in a pastel boilersuit.

Confusingly, kitsch cult objects will very often appeal to those same individuals who enthuse over the designer variety too. Valiant attempts were made to turn the wall-mounted flying china duck into a cult object. They foundered from over-exposure of too many facetious variations on the same theme. A more significant kitsch cult object is the famous motor car teapot from the 1930s, now available in reproduction form. A pinball table and a jukebox would also count. The Wurlitzer 1015 with the die castings and the arched bubble tube qualifies for sheer flamboyance. But the buffs make a strong case for the Seeburg M-100A. It was the first 100 selection machine – in jukebox terms, the key to the modern world.

The name cult shows some signs of abating, but it is still very strong in some areas. It was born originally as the result of a curious crossover from motor cars to clothes, then quickly spread to a wide variety of other products. Chromium plated signatures etched across the back of cars began to take on more and more significance from the 1950s. Initially, they were there to hint at the presence of an individual coach builder, carrying on a craft tradition. But they quickly became an essential part of the design, a flamboyant sign-off line forming an effective counterpoint to the tightly controlled architecture of the rest of the car. It also provided for the use of certain key cult words: currently it is 'Turbo', and '4x4'. In the past it was key initials – 'GT' used to be particularly popular. In the case of the Germans the message is codified to a string of numerals, witness the various BMW designations. The Italians and the British like names. The Americans are the most flamboyant with elaborate mascots. At some stage, this naming of names collided with the long established tradition of Mr Strauss and others in attaching a label in a visible position on the back of his garments. Some unknown genius brilliantly fused the two in one of the limited edition of Beetles with which Volkswagen celebrated the end of European production of the Führer's people's car. Denim seats, complete with a tag, and the word 'Jeans' painted on the outside of the door at ankle level were produced to be sold at a premium. Things got pretty much out of hand after this triumph. For a while, it was impossible to buy a blazer without alien initials over the buttons. And some sports manufacturers turned their wares into sandwich boards such was the enthusiasm with which they applied their insignia.

The idea, of course, was to create instant cult objects, ones which would convey with the minimum of effort the fact that their owners were people of taste and distinction. It got a message across all right, but not quite the one that was intended. All those initials and words and stripes radiate social insecurity with dazzling clarity. 'OK, so I buy my clothes at the right shop, but how will people know once I've taken them out of the bag?' In less sophisticated societies the answer is to wear your shirt inside out, so that passersby cannot fail to see the label.

One explanation for the rise of the name cult lies in its decorative role. Decoration and ornament of all kinds is taboo to orthodox modernist designers, frowned on as being 'dishonest', or frivolous, or even in one or two much quoted extreme cases, 'a crime'. And in a curious way, that attitude has percolated into the consciousness of the wider public who actually buy some of the products that the designers put their mark on. Products which are perceived as businesslike, professional, serious, masculine even, can't afford to be seen in willow patterns. They just don't look serious enough, although of course it's important to remember that a lot of those aforementioned 'serious' products are really nothing more than elaborate adult toys. But in many cases a box, serious though it may be, is just a box, indistinguishable from its rivals, and not appealing enough to get itself picked up off the shelf. It needs a little something extra to pep it up, a little decoration in fact. And the abstract pattern of a name can be used to do just that, without all the guilt problems or risks of making your product not look authentic enough. It can be done in an infinite variety of ways, anything from the spurious low budget utilitarianism of tea-chest stencil letters – look at the way the Sierra logo is handled on the back of the new Fords, at one extreme, to elaborately sculpted chrome lumps worked in contrasting shades of polished and brushed steel. What the words actually say is often much less important than how they're said. What counts is the chance a name provides for providing a little closet ornament.

The most conspicuous example is in the airline business, where just about everyone has exactly the same planes, fitted with the same seats – which are the same distance apart – travels at the same speed, and flies to the same places. All that's left to make your Boeing 747 seem different from everybody else's is to paint a name on the side.

You couldn't strictly call money a cult object. But examining what makes it seem like something worth more than the paper it's printed on can tell you quite a lot about cult objects. Everybody knows that a piece of paper isn't worth anything itself; but, even so, there is the watermark let into the fine quality paper, the crisp feeling of newly printed banknotes riffling through the fingers, the smell of the ink and the satisfying way that the engraved printing lets you actually feel the flourishes on the paper's surface with your thumb, all to build up a sense of expectation. All those properties go a long way to suspending

21

Right: Bringing a scent of rustic hearths, mellow quarry-tiled floors and oak beams to the kitchens of Finchley and Croydon, the Aga is still the quintessential focus of the home for the Volvo-driving classes

disbelief in the value of what's in your billfold. There's no doubt also that dollars, in particular, do look like *money*. They are in the first place green – clearly the colour of money, and they come with just the right amount of mystic symbolism on the back, in the shape of all those pyramids and magic eyes to provide a sense of the dramatic. American Express pulled off a really intelligent coup when they facelifted their plastic credit card with a new green design clearly inspired by the dollar bill. An American Express card probably does qualify as a cult object – think about the way you can loftily snap it down on hotel counters, and toss it into waiters' salvers – provided that you can be sure it's not going to bounce. But just compare the dollar with the Dutch guilder, a currency that has never recovered from an overdose of 1960s trendification which turned Dutch banknotes into gaudy, typographically tasteful cigarette coupons.

It's more difficult to analyse how a cult object is created than it is to identify one in action. Certain of them have the power to become the source of thinly coded messages, broadcasting to visitors what type of household they are in, or else they can pander to the obsessions of the household's members. Compare, for example, two different examples of such an apparently prosaic domestic object as the oven. Find an Aga in a British household, no matter how humble, and it will instantly place its owner as an aspirant to a very particular kind of wholesome rustic domesticity. It is the exact equivalent of parking a Volvo estate car outside the house, owning a Labrador, and baking your own bread. With its combination of heating and cooking functions, it is the earth goddess of suburbia, the last vestige of the hearth at the centre of a home. Its heavy, and antique enamelled outlines, and even heavier chambered doors, which swing shut with the ponderous majesty of a bank vault, contrive somehow to suggest the servants' hall of an Edwardian mansion. The problem for those who equip their homes with an Aga is that in reality it is none of these things, being originally a Swedish product, and named after the initials of the Svenska Akyiebolaget Gasacumulator, not the kind of mouthful that would go down too well in Finchley.

The diametric opposite of the Aga is the Neff, not exactly an object since it has to be built into a wall, but nevertheless, for a particular kind of home, just as significant a purchase as the Aga. Once it had the same touch of exotic stylishness, coupled with modernity, as the Citroën DS, but now it's slipped back a little to become part of the prawn cocktail good life.

Cult objects aren't tied to any one of these extremes, but they all have special qualities over and above what one could be entitled to expect from the simple considerations of performing a function.

Chapter Two

The joy of matt black

The world in black and white and Braun.
Why a Rolex is not about telling you the
time. How to carry your Filofax and when to
uncap your Mont Blanc

**Left: By the wafer-thin standards
of the Japanese, Braun's
calculator is technically as
obsolete as eight-track stereo.
But its Smartie-bright buttons
and finely chiselled matt black
body make it a pleasure to use all
the same**

On my desk as I write is a pocket calculator,
the Braun ET 22 to be precise. 'It means
Brown, and it is pronounced Brown', they
told me through gritted teeth at head office
in Frankfurt once, exasperated by the
English habit of rhyming Braun with lawn.
But the ET 22 – and with a name as
enigmatic as that, it could just as well be an
intercontinental ballistic missile as a
calculator – isn't brown at all. In fact it is
black, just like all the other Braun products
from electric toothbrushes to record players
that aren't finished in a shade of white. The
explanation for this singlemindedly
monochrome approach is that Dieter Rams,
Braun's design guru, has too delicate a
constitution to stomach anything more
demanding than black and white. So
distressing does he find the very idea of
visual disorder, that he has been known to
take a large paper bag with him on his
country walks, and return with it brim full
of salvaged rubbish picked up along the

way. You get the feeling that he would
develop a migraine from prolonged exposure
to a garden gnome. And that a drive down
the strip in Las Vegas could well prove
terminal.

Rams' office is a study in neutrality, the
Switzerland of the design world. It is the
kind of room in which a single fingerprint
on the wall, or a paper out of place on the
desk would have the impact of a klaxon
going off in the Reading Room of the British
Museum. He has designed everything in it:
the furniture, the products on the shelves,
the clock, the radio, the stereo and the
storage system. He is even responsible for
the building itself – part of a large complex
on the edge of Frankfurt's industrial
suburbs. And in the whole place, the only
splash of real colour comes from the orange
packet of cigarettes, permanently in Rams'
hands.

With the help of a room full of assistants
in matching Boris Karloff tunics and centre

partings, protected by locked corridor doors and security guards, Rams designs products for Braun that are reticent to the point of being invisible. 'They should be there, ready to perform effortlessly well when they are needed, but keep out of the way without imposing when they are not, just like an English butler,' he says. It is an attitude that has his marketing department worried. Like most marketing departments, they are not entirely convinced that good taste ever sold anything. They have already persuaded Rams to produce packaging that, while it doesn't actually shout, has at least raised its tone of voice above a whisper. And they are working on the monochrome business too. It may, or may not, do something for increasing Braun's sales, as its American parent company fervently hopes, but it is not a move that will go down very well with the legions of design buffs for whom Braun was once the matt black Valhalla of good taste.

In Britain, the marketing men don't believe that there is enough demand for the calculator to justify importing it at all, still less to promote it. Yet such is the word of mouth enthusiasm for it, that bootleg stocks are smuggled in and sold unofficially in the sort of shop patronized by BBC producers in search of pre-patched corduroy jackets and Eau Sauvage. In such settings, the ET 22 is treated with little short of religious devotion, a sacred piece of the True Plastic, floodlit and locked away behind glass.

But the Braun is far short of being the world's cleverest calculator. You can't even programme it. And it is bigger and more expensive than the credit card sized Japanese models that outperform it with ease. Now that you can put a personal computer that will keep a diary for you in your wallet, it is even something of a technological period piece. But it is still the supreme personal cult object in the sense that it becomes a constant presence. It will slip into a pocket, or fit into the hand, and inevitably it begins to affect its owner's mannerisms and the image that he projects to the world.

It is a toy of course, but like all the best toys, it looks convincing enough to be taken seriously. What is more, Rams has deliberately designed the ET 22 to make the most of its potential for play. He has created a series of rituals around its use, in the way that smokers tapping a cigarette on the packet, and lighting it, hands cupped against the wind, have rituals. Above all, it is good to touch. Running your fingers over the ultra-precise mouldings, and the shiny control buttons, bright as Smarties, is as soothing as playing with worry beads. It comes in a flexible pouch that is meant to protect the keys. Moulded out of decidedly uncissy grainy black plastic, its hefty welts make it look like a cigar case. It is the only calculator that you can slip into your top pocket, engineer style in the way that the slide rule, which it has replaced as the technocrat's badge of office, used to be. Ironically, of course, it isn't real technocrats who have made such a fetish out of the ET 22, but the design groupies with an eye for its looks.

The top of the case is cut away to reveal a winsome sliver of the calculator itself, looking as sharp as an automatic in a shoulder holster, and showing off to advantage a flash of finely chiselled ribbing that provides a grip. Pull out the calculator between forefinger and thumb – remember how pulp private eyes were always stripteasing a packet of gum – and you are dealing with a solid presence. The calculator is properly proportioned for the hand, and it feels reassuringly like a slate that you can work on with chalk, rather than some alien piece of microcircuitry. The keys are generously sized buttons, floating free of the matt black surface beneath, and are colour coded by function, for Rams is prepared to countenance using colour when he has an excuse that will not trouble his Calvinist conscience.

Black is for the ordinary numerals, brown is for the command keys: multiplication, square roots, and so on. And a single blob of yellow is reserved for the all-important equals key. The on-off switch is different again, with a side-to-side movement and an accompanying click that lets you know for sure that you haven't left it on by mistake and are draining the battery. Turn the whole thing over, and you find four soft rubber feet, sprouting from the back of the case. They are there to ensure that the calculator won't simply slide off the tracing paper on your drawing board. The composition is completed by the prewar simplicity of the Braun logo, which appears on both calculator and case. In a word, it is perfection. What Rams has done is to create an identity for what was, when he designed it back in 1977, still a relatively new type of machine. There were no rules about how a calculator should look, nothing comparable with the mental picture that we all carry of what 'the house', or 'the car' looks like. In the past, designers would have taken their cue from how a machine functioned. But a calculator is not the same as a steam engine, say, for it has precious few moving parts, and it is possible to arrange its circuits in practically any configuration you want. There was, as yet, no appropriate image for calculators. Should they be made to look like serious scientific instruments in gunmetal grey, or should they be finished in tinsel and glitter like children's toys? Rams kept clear of both extremes, and created a convincing expression of what the calculator *ought* to look like.

Small wonder that it has become an essential personal accessory, even for people who would never dream of adding up a column of figures in public. Left suggestively on your desk, it starts transmitting all kinds of flattering signals. It can even perform as a discreet kind of

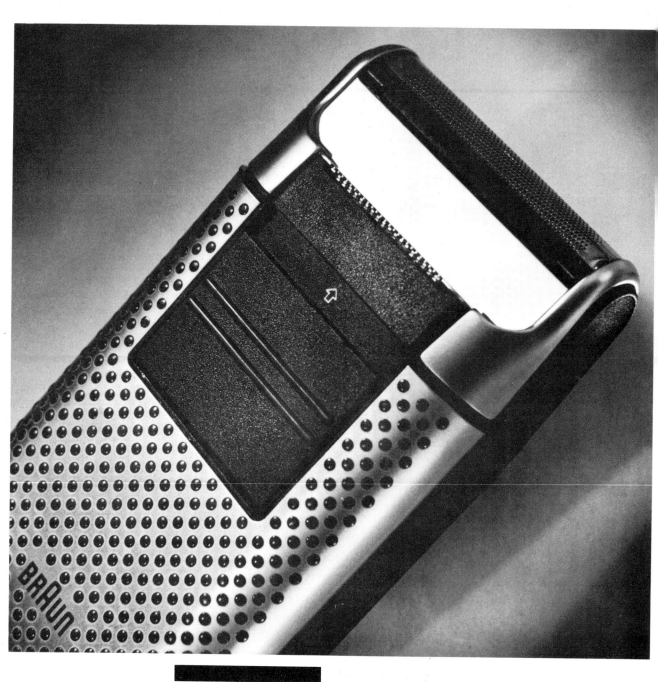

28

personal jewellery. If only Rams had been able to do something about the typography. What goes on the keys is refined enough, but the liquid crystal display flashes up the usual illiterate digital typeface.

Thanks to Rams, Braun has a number of products that qualify as cult objects. Apart from the calculator, there is the HT 1 toaster, designed by Reinhold Weiss in 1961, which inspired the artist Richard Hamilton to embark on a whole series of tributes to Braun. Rams's Mactron lighter produced in 1971 is pitched at the opposite extreme from the Zippo. The Mactron is smooth, suave and slim. At the lightest of touches it will produce a precision controlled lick of blue flame. The Zippo, on the other hand, is nature in the raw. It needs brute force and muscle to persuade it into action, and trails a reek of fuel oil as strong as a DC 10's wherever it goes. The Mactron is for effete sophisticates who don't want to spoil the line of their suit. The Zippo is for craggy battered types with hearts of gold and trench coats. But Braun is best known for its family of electric shavers, and what better example of a personal cult object could there be? Nearly half the adult population submit themselves to a daily shaving ritual of some kind. Braun have elevated the equipment for these rites to the status of works of art, most recently in the shape of the Micron Universal. It is carved from satisfyingly heavy steel with a vaguely surgical feel. Teams of Braun

scientists spent years working out how to coat its lissom brushed metal body with black rubber dots, a feat more difficult than you might imagine. The ostensible explanation for all this effort was the quest to provide the shaver with a better grip on his machine. In fact, of course, the point was to allow Braun to deploy simultaneously two of the most effective lures in the designer's repertoire. The Micron boasts not just the obvious glitter of chrome, but the newer hook of matt black as well. This is known as covering all the angles.

At one time Braun used to promote the Micron with a remarkable television commercial that cut rapidly back and forth between close-ups of the business end of the shaver ploughing its way through the mountainous landscape of the chin, and a black Porsche 911 negotiating thickets of stubble. Superficially the message it was meant to put across was that this was a shaver faster and more surefooted than those of the competition. But what the commercial was really doing was making a parallel between two different types of cult object, the Porsche and the Micron.

Intriguingly, Rams himself drives just such a Porsche, a little out of character one might think for so steadfastly serious a designer. Even more intriguingly, the Porsche 911's designer, the grandson of Professor Ferdinand Porsche, he of the Beetle, is himself the author of a couple of highly successful cult objects that have something in common with the Rams approach. Porsche was a student at the Ulm design school, the last bastion of the Bauhaus less-is-more approach. Rams taught there, so it is not surprising to find that they share a certain missionary zeal.

'A correct product,' claims Porsche, with the controlled hysteria of the true believer, 'means many things.' To name but a few it means, 'control of the assembly of single parts, functional design of the contents in favour of exterior aesthetics, realism in perceiving what is possible, concentration of all efforts on the trends of an achievable future, not utopian speculation, development of new techniques to satisfy potential users, and last, but not least, a sincere team spirit to accumulate a genuine specialized know how.' Quite. Now even allowing for certain losses in the translation, and for the po-faced seriousness with which so many designers take themselves – and who but a designer could talk about a 'correct product' – this is going a bit far.

After all, what Porsche has been doing since falling out with the rest of the family is to create such vital contributions to Western civilization as designer sunglasses, wristwatches and executive briefcases. Yet these aforementioned sunglasses, wristwatches and briefcases come on as strong as kidney dialysis machines and mainframe computers.

Porsche will tell you that he prefers to talk about the philosophy of an object, rather than its style. 'Each product has its own particular needs, criteria and codes, which must be kept separate and not confused. Consequently, a clock, intended as a precision instrument, may have a black dial, with numbers in white for clearer reading, while a telephone in a private room has no reason for being black.'

This is the prop that Porsche, Rams, and other latterday functionalists always fall back on. They tell you, flying in the face of all the evidence, that they have no style, just a rational approach. Yet when you examine the real reasons that prompt people to buy the products they design, their motivations are seldom as highminded or as rational as their designers – to say nothing of the Consumers' Association – would like to think.

There is no rational reason for buying a £700 Porsche Design wristwatch which has no less than four separate dials, a calendar, a stopwatch, and looks like the flight deck of a Boeing, if all you want to do is to make sure that you aren't late for the occasional appointment. We are back in the territory of the Jeep in the supermarket carpark again.

The point of all this excess capacity is partly to massage the ego of the owner and partly to tell other people something about him or her. The super-precision delineations around the dial that go down to fifths of a second are frankly decorative. The two business-like studs set into the rim of the

Right: Micro millisecond accuracy is spectacularly redundant if you are simply worried about keeping the occasional appointment. But it does give Porsche Design the chance to use all those super-precise delineations as a sophisticated kind of ornament

case are there to maximize the play value of the watch. The message that the Porsche carries is not simply about conspicuous consumption. After all, if the possession of large quantities of raw money is what you are trying to put across, there is always the possibility of buying one of those little creations fashioned from pieces of gold bullion, where the watch face is stamped with the assay mark of a Swiss bank, and the strap all but comes with a diamond studded price tag.

The Porsche is for those who think they are clued up enough to keep away from mere vulgar display, but who still aren't entirely confident about their own taste. The logo on the dial is discreet, but still prominent enough to reassure those who believe that initials speak louder than words. And, for those casual acquaintances who might not know quite what the two squiggles loosely representing the letters p and d really mean, the message is underscored by spelling out the words Porsche Design in full.

Real design buffs, however, go in for obscurity in their choice of wristwatch. They may choose muscular black plastic from Lip, sadly no longer available, or anorexic monochrome from Georg Jensen, or the remarkable Bulova Accutron, the world's first quartz watch, which has had its face dissected to reveal its green and orange entrails, and which adorns even such defiantly unmodish wrists as that of James Stirling, most formidable of Britain's contemporary architects. The original 1926 Rolex Oyster has also come to occupy a special position, spanning the divide between plain expensive and designer taste. Between them Ian Fleming and James Bond, these unsurpassed masters of the art of creating cult objects, made the Rolex into something special, along with the shaken but not stirred Martini. And now the process has been completed with Rolexes from the 1950s receiving the ultimate accolade of a special sale at Sotheby's where they attracted higher prices than can be commanded by identical contemporary models.

There's no doubt about it, the Rolex *is* butch. Oyster is about the right word for it – it claimed to be the first of the waterproofs, but its status quotient has fluctuated wildly in the face of the ploy popular with the design crowd of aspiring to the common touch. What more effective putdown of those who wear their bank balance on their wrist can there be than the flaunting of a no-nonsense cheap and cheerful Timex Mercury 20521, or a Casio Digital – note incidentally the way in which Timex, which used to be called the United States Time Corporation cashed in on the 'ex' suffix.

All these watches are as much about sending out carefully judged identity signals as they are about telling the time. Some are capable of conveying fine shades of meaning,

Right: Bulova was so proud of its high-tech quartz watch in the 1960s that it dissected the face to reveal its innards in all their green and orange glory. Now long out of production, enthusiasts have banded together to form owners' clubs to swop precious spare parts

34

others can only shriek headlines. The Porsche wristwatch falls into the former category. It says one thing, but means another. It aspires to matt-black designer-speak, but in mint condition, at least, it is *the* watch of the après-ski crowd, and is destined for the wrists of those hardfaced beauties whose annual migrations between Caribbean beaches and Alpine chalets mark the passing of the seasons. They are watches for people who bristle zips and jumpsuits and leather trousers: people, moreover, who believe that while a Roller spells new money a Mercedes means style.

The Porsche has been so successful at tapping this lucrative and upwardly mobile market that other manufacturers have resorted to desperate measures to wrest away a share. Ferrari is the latest name being taken in vain. It is now coupled with a watch design, gaudy as a neon sign, that would undoubtedly give poor Dieter Rams apoplexy. Its face is scored with a grid of brass so ostentatious that it looks like an old-time diver's helmet. And the strap is in understated red, blue and gold. Here is a watch that is an attempt to create a cult object by reshuffling the components of two genuine cults, the Porsche and the Cartier Tank watch, changing the colour scheme, and hoping for the best. It does not succeed.

Eyewear, as it is called these days, offers dramatic possibilities for those who want to use their possessions to work for their image. Long before the arrival of all those so-called designer frames gratuitously embellished with initials worked into the frame, the classical age of spectacle design was dominated by the Euclidian splendour of those remarkable gloss black perfect circles that were worn first by Le Corbusier, and which have represented the mark of aspiring architectural big-leaguers ever since. You have to be *very* serious even to attempt wearing them. They go with severe dark suits, black ties and designing opera houses, not tweed jackets and kitchen extensions. They bestow an instant air of erudition, suggestive of prolonged exposure to central European academies and Viennese coffee houses. The frames are flat, the side pieces do not hook, they just sweep majestically back over the ears.

High tech came early to spectacles, with the once revolutionary aviator sunglasses: large metal frames, stiffened by a welded crossbar and twin nose bridges in clear plastic – a classic case of an exposed structure being used to decorative effect, just like the high tech architecture of the early 1980s. Like so many design icons, aviator specs were originally intended for military use – in this case for the pilots of the U.S. Army Air Corps in the 1930s. It is hard to overestimate the influence of militaria on design in general, and cult objects in particular. It can be explained partly by the sheer quantity of money and the effort that is invested in military research and development budgets: the

Left: As much a part of arch-cultist James Bond's essential equipment as a shaken, not stirred, Martini, the Rolex Oyster has gone through a series of incarnations since it first appeared in 1926, but its butch good looks have always stood for snobbery with violence

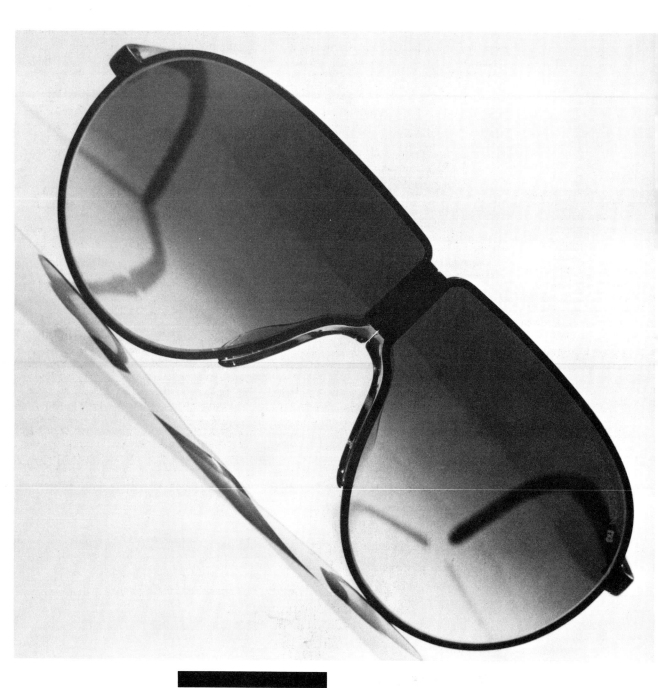

36

military do at least have the chance to get things right, although they don't always manage it. There is also, however, the uncomfortable power and fascination exercised by gunmetal glamour. Uniforms easily become a fetish, and weapons have a special fascination to do with the power that they can bestow. Military design, we assume too easily, is purely functional, that is to say, design shorn of the sell factor, and designed for maximum utility and efficiency in the most rugged of conditions. That is, of course, an illusion. Fashion is just as much a part of design for the military as it is for anybody else. And it is the winning sides that are the most fashionable. Look at the way in which the Prussian-style helmet swept the world to the exclusion of the kepi after the Franco-Prussian war of the 1870s. Weapons and uniforms are designed to look intimidating. It is a tradition that links the Polaris submarine with the Viking longship.

The original version of those aviator shades had gold frames – nothing was too good for our boys – and green glass lenses. More recent versions have gone down the mirror-glass road to achieve the singularly hostile anonymity that is beloved by secret police forces the world over, especially by those who place greater store on intimidation than on concealment.

Porsche Design's Carrera sunglasses owe a lot to aviators. Their lenses have the same teardrop shape as the original, albeit more refined and curvaceous, and the exoskeleton frames are in matt black, naturally. The frame is hinged to allow the whole thing to fold up like an insect, into little more than the space taken by just one lens, and slip into a little black purse destined for the pockets of, presumably, muscle-bound types shinning up the masts of expensive yachts, or even hired assassins with high-powered rifles. But doubts are raised about the man of action image by the bizarre innovation of etching the words Porsche Design across the lenses themselves. It creates an effect not unlike that of an expensive tennis star who goes out on the centre court at Wimbledon wearing her sponsor's colours, or the name of a cigarette company worked into her skirt. Except, of course, that in the case of the sunglasses, it is the happy consumer who is paying handsomely for the privilege of carrying the magic word, Porsche, carved into his forehead.

The fountain pen offers rich possibilities as a cult object. There is after all so much more that you can do with one, than with a wristwatch say. The watch is stuck more or less permanently under your shirt cuff. The fountain pen is in quite a different league. You can choose to show it off, defiantly sporting a row of pens in a front pocket to demonstrate a healthy respect for learning. Or else you can use the inside pocket: handy for a quiet but confident statement about your sense of taste when you are reaching for your cheque book. Ring the changes

38

with pens clipped to the side of a tie, or in the V-neck of a pullover. For hard cases there is the possibility of a specially created pen pocket: in boilersuits, or those quasi-military shirts that come with a built-in lashing for securing rolled up sleeves in the face of the enemy. Pens have about them the basics of a language of social and stylistic ambition before we have even touched on the hardware itself, which further extends the vocabulary.

The artificially archaic Mont Blanc represents one extreme. The firm makes a whole range of pens, from slim, cylindrical ballpoints to conventional, sleek fountain pens. But the Meisterstuck Diplomat, as it is known, is the only one of their models to qualify as a cult object. The attention to detail is extraordinary: Diplomats have all the elaboration of Latin-American banknotes. The word Meisterstuck is carved in fist-deep letters in the gold band around the cap, and cross-hatched to fool the counterfeiters. There are two versions, varying in size. The 148 is large, the 149 is simply vast. Obviously there is a whimsical streak somewhere in the Mont Blanc organization: amid the baroque flourishes on the 14-carat nib is inscribed, in the cramped hand of a Prussian bank clerk, the number 4810, the height in metres of the eponymous mountain peak.

The pen's bulk offers plenty of scope for intimidatory manoeuvres in the course of those diplomatic confrontations that it contrives to suggest it was designed for. You can fiddle with the top at difficult moments, or else, with the studied deliberation that one assumes comes naturally to the representatives of Her Britannic Majesty, unscrew the top and fix it to the end of the pen furthest from the nib, in so doing, inflating its proportions to the scale of a baton. The latter is often a useful gambit, as Lech Walesa, who signed the Solidarity agreements with the Polish government using a six-foot monster Biro, could tell you.

The Mont Blanc, with its antique pretensions, has always been a reactionary design. Far more adventurous is the Parker 51, a landmark among fountain pens that did for the Parker Pen Company of Jamesville, Wisconsin, what the Sydney Opera House did for Australia. Its sleek gallic curves suggest the Citroën DS 19 of the 1950s so strongly that it comes as a surprise to be reminded that the 51 was produced as early as 1939 to celebrate Parker's fifty-first anniversary. Did they, one can't help wondering, decide to put as brave a face as they could on coming in a year late on the $250,000 development programme?

The 51 is sleek and streamlined, its barrel narrowing to a pointed hood that swoops low and protectively over the nib. The cap is brushed steel, and adorned with a flamboyant arrow-shaped clip, straying for a moment into the field of representation

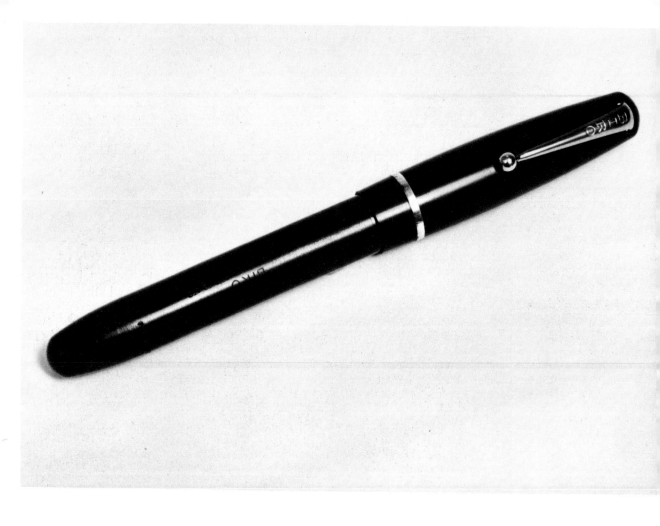

40

after the abstracted form of the rest of the pen. Inside is a metal framework, holding a specially formulated synthetic rubber ink sac – quick drying inks tended to rot the natural variety. You squeeze the sac between finger and thumb, which does away with the need for the cumbersome lever action devices, that clutter many of the 51's contemporaries.

With such a pioneering design, almost as bold a leap as the jump from cut-throat to safety razors, it is surprising that it took Parker as long as it did to move into ballpoints. It wasn't until 1954 that the company came up with a challenge to the virtual monopoly held by Bic. What is now such a humble and ubiquitous object should not be underestimated. It was, after all, at one time second only to denim as the Western item most sought-after by the indefatigable black marketeers behind the Iron Curtain. It was originally designed

...ft: Biro patented the ballpoint ...n. Although still styled to look ...e a conventional fountain pen, ...remained a high priced rarity, ...til Bic turned it into a mass-...oduced cut-price item

...ght: First sold in 1939, the ...rker 51 – produced for the ...mpany's fifty-first ...niversary – has curves that are ...distinctive and timeless as a ...troën DS 19. No less a luminary ...an Laszlo Moholy-Nagy waxed ...rical about its shape

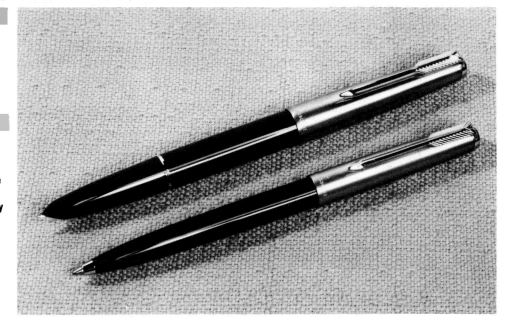

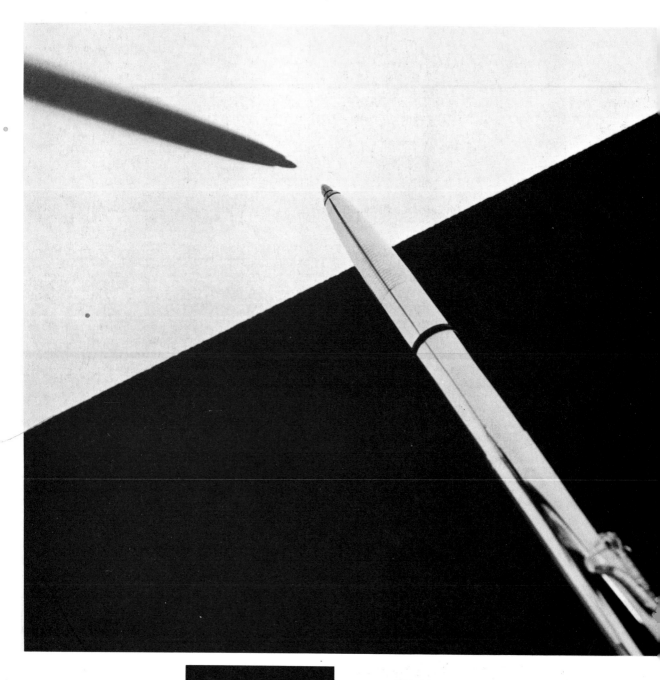

42

with military applications in mind, to work at altitudes at which fountain pens could not function in unpressurized aircraft cockpits. The trick of the ballpoint was in getting the consistency of the ink right, smooth enough to keep it flowing but not so moist that it would pour out over your zoot suit, or flying jacket, as the case might be. The trick was first perfected by the Hungarian emigré Lazlo Biro, who patented the first Biro pen in 1938 when he reached Argentina. It was the wily Frenchman Marcel Bich, however, who was the first to reap really substantial rewards from Biro's invention. He took Biro's very expensive product, and marketed it in a way that brought prices tumbling down, thanks to a low-budget, mass-produced design, in much the way that cheap digital watches of the late 1970s changed the picture twenty years later.

If the Biro was *the* pen of the jet age, the Fisher Space Pen aspires to the same role in the astronaut era. And the way in which it is now proudly marketed by its inventor, Paul Fisher, offers a glimpse of the glamour that the Biro once must have possessed.

Mr Fisher is a man with one of those crewcuts favoured by Polish scientists, and his portrait adorns the advertising for his pens. He proudly boasts of having spent $1m researching the problem of producing a pen that will write under completely weightless conditions – for most of us, surely, the most redundant capability of all. Yet it must be admitted that there is a

certain charm to the idea, even though the humble pencil could do the task just as well.

Ordinary ballpoints rely on gravity to feed ink to the business end of the pen. They have a vent in the barrel to allow air to replace ink in the reservoir as it is used up, allowing the ink to evaporate, and sometimes to leak all over the pen's owner. The Fisher Pen, on the other hand, to ensure that you are able to travel boldly where no fountain pen has gone before, is nitrogen- rather than air-powered. That is to say, Fisher's Pen has a sealed ink cartridge, in which specially formulated visco elastic – like chewing gum, dummy – ink is under pressure from nitrogen gas at 50 psi. This pushes ink through to the ballpoint under just about any conditions. It will write at any angle, even pointing upwards. It will write under water, or at 50 degrees below freezing point. What is more, the shelf life is 100 years, and it will write for three miles without running out.

As Mr Fisher points out, not only did NASA use it for the moon landings as standard issue, but the Soviets bought it for the Soyuz programme, too. With all this heavy credibility going for it, the Fisher would be a cult object whatever it looked like. But Fisher's design helps the whole process along. It looks like the sort of pen that isn't a pen, but which conceals those gadgets that James Bond types use to attach themselves to ceilings, or to communicate with passing helicopters. It's sleek, silver,

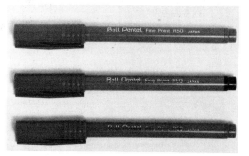

very heavy, and undoubtedly otherworldly. In short, Mr Fisher seems to have the last word in the super-redundant pen. Mind you, if the thing ever did fail on a space shuttle, the cost of shipping it back to Forest Park, Illinois, to cash in on the lifetime replacement guarantee makes it unlikely that Mr Fisher will have much to worry about.

The Fisher hasn't yet lost the cult status that the Biro once had, but cheap and cheerful disposable pens received a boost from the Japanese in the 1970s. Pentel's blocky, green barrelled, plastic ballpoint design, which followed its production of the world's first fibretip in 1960, almost became a cult. It didn't quite pull it off, probably because it didn't make for an agreeable enough writing action, but it was a creditable try. The Rotring technical drawing pen does qualify for full cult status, however. Outside the drawing office or designer's studio, its hypodermic needle of

a nib, fashioned from stainless steel, and capability of delivering a steady and precis black line within an accuracy limit of 0.1 o a millimetre, represents more than sufficie redundant capacity for any cult object. It also manages to tap an even stronger cult theme, the magpie collector's instinct.

The Rotring comes in colour coded sets, with an engraved stripe set into the gloss black barrel, showing you the size of the nib. Developed in Germany after the Secon World War, the earliest Rotrings came in a fountain-pen style configuration, complete with a brass clip – to attach it to the pocke of your overalls, presumably. Nowadays, these have been replaced with little screw caps. A Rotring's rightful place is on the drawing board, but with a little coaxing they can be persuaded to produce a spider scrawl that approximates to handwriting.

The Filofax is another personal cult objec that taps the magpie instinct. It is based o a system that could not be simpler, a ring binder that lets you combine an address book with a diary, and constantly allows fo updates of the contents without discarding the elements that you need to keep. Aficionados can create a complete world of well-regimented order within the secure black Morocco leather covers of a Filofax. While all around all are losing their heads, the Filofax owner can rest secure in the calm of his graphs, his tables, his dates and his compulsive list-making.

The idea came from America, where a

Right: It's not what you keep inside your Filofax that really matters, it's the way you carry it that marks you out from the crowd—brandished across the chest for maximum effect, or tucked under the arm for the discreet

46

similar system was called the Lefax. It arrived in Britain in a refined form in the 1930s, and smouldered quietly for several decades before bursting out into fully fledged cult status in the 1970s. It is the essential accessory for graphic designers, journalists and media persons of all persuasions. The Filofax has come to take on the characteristics of a handbag; slip in a cheque book, buy a flap to take your credit cards, and there is room for everything. That is what has made it into a real cult object. People develop their own particular way of carrying their Filofax. Clutching it tightly across the chest or cradled in the crook of the arm are both popular variations. But the classic mode is to hold it clamped in the hand like a semaphore flag. The Filofax was originally innocent of any corrupting intervention from design. Its shape and form were the artless product of a commercial mind. Perhaps as a result, its presence and its image are all the stronger. It is available in a variety of formats, in a range that goes from the basic minimum to an elaborate double spine version. The Europeans have a tiny version in which the ring binders are too close together, creating the same dubious impression as men with eyebrows that meet in the middle.

The simple boyish charm of the Swiss Army penknife, so called, has a similar origin to that of the Filofax. That is to say it is popular with children of all ages, in the same way that the Meccano set once was.

And, like that period piece from the 1950s, it is possible to begin one's obsession for the Swiss Army penknife in a small way, say with just a couple of folding blades, and then to become entirely hooked, working up to the 18 option special, which boasts such essential ingredients of the Swiss national deterrent as nail files, wire strippers and that nameless thing for taking stones out of horses' hooves. Finished in bright scarlet, and proudly emblazoned with the silver cross of Helvetia, Swiss Army knives have done sterling service from the Himalayas – where mountaineer Doug Scott used one to sort out an ice-clogged oxygen pipe before commencing his final assault on Everest – to Vietnam. In South-east Asia, the Swiss Army knife became an unofficial part of GI issue, thanks to its helpful capacity to sort out the perennial problem of the jamming M16 rifle.

The penknife is made by a Swiss company with the suitably martial name of Victorinox – it was named after Victoria, wife of the founder, Carl Elsener. Victorinox is still a family firm, run by Elsener's descendants, all called Carl, ever since 1884. The firm produces all kinds of cutlery, but it is still the Army knife – so named by the British, although the Swiss Army takes only about 80,000 or so of the annual production of around 4,000,000 a year – that occupies pride of place in the company. Elsener patented the Offiziermesser in June 1897. In those days it had two blades, a tin opener,

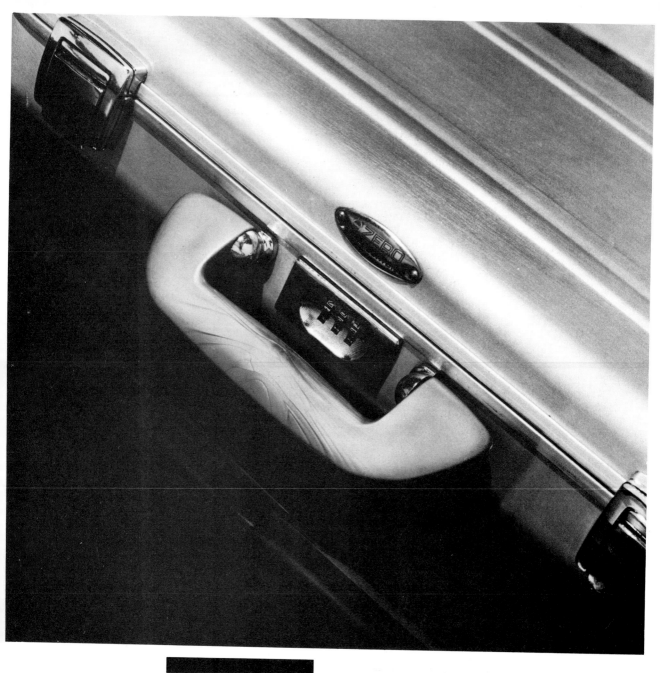

48

a corkscrew, and a punch. Since then there have been more than a hundred model variations, most of which are still in production, ranging from the *Bijou,* destined for the handbag, and well equipped with nail files, to the authentic cult status hulking Champion, which boasts 16 blades, and no less than 24 different functions, including tweezers, magnifying glass and toothpick.

Luggage is probably the most important personal cult object of all. It arrives ahead of you at strange hotels where your credit is in doubt, and at other people's homes where you must make an instant good impression at house parties. You carry it on to aeroplanes, and stand next to it at railway stations. It is an essential part of establishing that you are a person of substance in strange places, almost in the way that a car or a house can provide you with credentials, but luggage is rather more portable than either.

Cult luggage, however, since the demise of the Gladstone bag, begins and ends with Mr Halliburton, Louis Vuitton is for the vulgar; Samsonite, especially the matt black variety with the bright red Golf-inspired stripe is even worse. Halliburton, on the other hand – according to the legend, an oil engineer in the Mid-West – was responsible for creating what might not be the most practical piece of luggage that the world has ever seen, but what is certainly one of the most stylish.

Halliburton's original idea was to create a case that could stand up to the rough and tumble of drilling rig life. And he did it with a solid aluminium design that is as curvaceous, and about as tough, as a dodgem car. The trouble with it is, of course, that though a Halliburton case will stand up to being run over by a juggernaut, it is almost too heavy to lift even when it is empty. Solid aluminium was just the thing, however, for the metalworking companies looking for peacetime alternatives to the aircraft production that had kept them going during World War Two. So it was that Halliburton took his invention to the Zero Corporation of Burbank, California, who now make it in a large range of sizes. Zero push the Halliburton as a product of semi-mystical significance with a geometry that would have won the heart of the purest of the Bauhaus pure. 'To experienced travellers, form follows function,' burbles the leaflet that accompanies every case. 'Particularly when it comes to luggage. They travel first class, and they expect that their belongings travel first class too.'

The Halliburton is closer, however, in its streamlined shape, its sparkling plastic handles, and the ribbed profile of its sides to the spirit of the Deco 1920s. It is a must for any architect with high tech pretensions, despite the fearsome price tag. They all tell you that they picked it up cheap in Hong Kong. But, in fact, they paid far too much for it in Harrods.

Left: For all its streamlined curves, Halliburton's aluminium shell briefcase is worryingly heavy, even when it's empty. But that hasn't stopped its aficionados from investing in the intimidating credibility that it bestows

Chapter Three

Essential objects

What the well-dressed desk is wearing.
Where to put your Rolodex. The typewriter
for poets; the meaning of luggage, and the
campaign for real radios

Left: If you can persuade people to buy a tape recorder that doesn't record, and that is only intelligible through headphones, then you can clearly persuade them to buy anything. Having performed the trick once, Sony have been able to go on capitalizing on the success of the Walkman, most notably with the 'sports' model, finished in deep-sea-diver yellow, and set off with squishy rubber-covered controls

Gadgets are there to make it easier to do the things that you never dreamed that you wanted to. That is to say, hardly essential to everyday survival on a desert island, but, on the other hand, capable of making you feel a little better on rainy afternoons. You don't, for example, really need a watch with a bleeper that gives you, and the next three rows in the cinema, audible proof every time it passes the quarter hours. But it is a trick that appeals to a certain mentality. Presumably, it is something to do with the feeling that it could be a functional bleep, the mark of an individual really in demand – a brain surgeon on call for an emergency, perhaps.

Electrically powered carving knives, programmable door chimes, or the kind of gas-powered corkscrew inspired by the Bulgarian secret service technique for despatching foes with jet-propelled poison-tipped umbrellas are of little practical use. Yet great ingenuity and effort is expended on their production. And, more to the point, people go out and buy them. What is happening is that the forces which create authentic cult objects are being harnessed to sell products that flatter their owners. It may be by giving a spurious professional look to a kitchen utensil, or by making a device which feels good to touch and to use, or simply by facelifting a mundane product so that it looks better.

The most successful gadgets naturally become cult objects themselves, and the reverse is true only occasionally. What must be, by any definition, one of the most successful gadgets of all time, however, the Sony Walkman, is very definitely a cult object.

What could have been a more brilliant marketing coup than persuading millions of people all around the world that they wanted to buy a tape recorder which couldn't record? This was the real stroke of genius associated with the Walkman, not the marginal technical refinements needed to perfect personal stereo. Well, perhaps it would be more accurate to describe a Walkman as fairly personal stereo.

Blissfully rapt devotees wander the streets, quite unaware of the tinkly curtain of sound that they radiate in all directions from their spongy orange headphones. Presumably they will be equally blissful on the day when someone in Tokyo pulls a switch, and the world's armies of Walkman wearers swivel eastward and march into the sea like remote controlled androids.

Sony's triumph lay in its ability to package the Walkman in a form that was not only capable of being carried around strapped to the body, but which also looked at home when it was. Tiny orange headphones clip over the ears like jewellery, a matt grey flex snakes down towards the waist, and, above all, the box itself, with its winking lights and wedge-shaped controls, all made the Walkman into a cult object, one that has sold in millions.

It is being able to marshal that combination of skills that has made Sony a success, and not surprisingly the company is equally accomplished at putting about slightly misleading stories about the birth of the Walkman to help the process along. One version spread by Sony was that the company's dynamic chairman, Akio Morita, had the first set knocked up so that he could listen to classical music while he played tennis. A slightly more convincing version had him plugging together a Walkman prototype using a small player, and headphones, to keep him going on long haul flights.

The Walkman was a calculated attempt by Sony's tape recorder division to shift more product at a time when it was faced with declining sales in a market that was already saturated. Their strategy of developing a new product succeeded brilliantly. Two million units had been sold within 18 months of the Walkman's 1979 launch, and all the other Japanese manufacturers struggled to jump on the bandwagon.

A race to produce ever smaller Walkmen, and Walkmen-inspired tape players, broke out. Very quickly the machines were shrinking to less than the size of the tape cassette itself. And now even that barrier has been breached, with the bizarre return of the open reel to reel tape player, using miniature reels the size of small coins, which you can carry around with you to slip into a cassette type player.

It is an astonishing step backward into inconvenient convenience, bearing in mind that the tape cassette originally triumphed over the open reel precisely because it was such a convenient alternative. But then it is no more extraordinary a development than the plethora of Walkman accessories that are now available. These include clip-on speakers, and even graphic equalizers – devices that are supposed to give high quality sound reproduction, but have your belt hanging with as many bandoliers and equipment pouches as a Sandinista guerrilla with a rocket-propelled grenade launcher on his back.

The Walkman went through a rapid series of model changes after the launch of the primitive WM 1. The WM 2 is the definitive model now, in grey, with the matt black WM 3 a more elaborately design-conscious alternative.

The most cult conscious version is the Sports Walkman which comes in a bright yellow casing that is clearly intended to signal 'waterproof' diver's equipment. However, if you read the small print on the box, you discover that it will just about withstand a gentle splashing, and no more. But no matter, who can resist the vivid dashes of post-modern colour on the two triangular controls, and the squishy rubber membrane that protects the switches? So quickly has the Walkman progressed up the evolutionary tree, that the sports model may well be a dead end, a freak left stranded by atrophying interest in the same way as that dinosaur of portable stereo, the ghetto blaster.

In sheer noise and aggression, the ghetto blaster is the ultimate deterrent, all about territory and turf. The Walkman, on the other hand, is just as arrogant, and hostile, but not so outwardly aggressive. A Walkman is suggesting 'I'm not really here,' in the same way that mirrored sunglasses do.

The ghetto blaster was butch. You have to be tough to lift those things. They are as big as a suitcase, and come covered in knobs, dials and chrome. The Walkman is introverted, neurotic, and more upmarket, but could never replace the ghetto blaster in the affections of real enthusiasts.

In Japanese corporate hierarchy, it is a paradoxical fact that the designer rates pretty close to rock bottom, attracting as much prestige as the lowliest of draughtsmen. When you try to ask Sony who *designed* the Walkman, they scratch their heads and look puzzled. They have, after all, a whole studio of people adept at turning out any conceivable styling package to order. As the years have gone by, the Sonys, the Aiwas and the Hitachis have become more and more skilled at picking up on early tremors of change in the market's style language, and synthesizing them in a convincing way.

So far, it has always been the West that has been the original source of the design looks that the Japanese put across. It was Sony's expertise in recycling teak veneer and chrome on to their Trinitrons that helped them cut a swathe through the Western television market. In the early days of hifi, Sony were quick to latch on to the fact that what sold was the scientific look. So they built component systems, with speaker, amp and deck each as aggressively different as possible, to suggest a high tech lash-up created by a longhaired Ph.D. from

California, along with all the brushed chrome that the heart could wish for.

Once the first joys of chrome began to die, the Japanese were quick to change tack, producing instead cool matt black miniaturized systems. And now they are churning out cheerful pastel hues, whose underlying message is of a sufficient confidence in the product to take the performance of high technology equipment for granted. That is to be secure enough to decorate the product in toylike colours, safe in the knowledge that nobody will take it for a toy.

Ettore Sottsass, veteran Italian designer, was doing exactly the same thing back in the 1960s, when he designed the Valentine typewriter for Olivetti. The idea was to turn out a machine that had nothing in common with the huge gunmetal grey tyrants that ruled the office at that time, but which would, instead, as Sottsass put it, 'keep amateur poets company on quiet Sunday mornings in the country, or provide a highly coloured object on a table in a studio apartment', presumably like some kind of flower arrangement.

You *can* type with the Valentine. But that isn't really the point, which is just as well, because as a typewriter, the Valentine leaves a lot to be desired. The keys won't take much of a pounding, and the mechanism is a trifle tinny. But if you bought one, you had the compensation of owning a machine in which play value has quite deliberately

been made much of. The plastic case, and the slip-on carrying cover are both bright red, while the ribbon spools are equipped with even more vivid orange dots, 'like the two eyes of a robot', as Sottsass puts it, gnomic as ever. Smart young Italians were to be seen carrying Valentines on promenades of Milan's Galleria, just as ten years before they were showing off their Lambrettas.

Even more beautiful than the Valentine is a later product from Olivetti, the Lexikon. This was, as Olivetti proudly boasted at the time, the 'world's first portable golfball typewriter'. The fact that it makes a dreadful noise, and that after more than 30 minutes of continuous use, the keys become distinctly mutinous about delivering even type, and that it is about as portable as a telephone box, did nothing to stop design buffs taking to the Lexikon instantly.

And to be fair, for all its technical drawbacks, Mario Bellini's design *is* beautiful. Its curves are lush and voluptuous. Its contours are sleek and subtle, so much so that Bellini has a disconcerting way of demonstrating his work with slides interspersed with nude photographs. The Lexikon comes in quiet, but sharp colours – a dark grey body, set off with pillar box red rollers at each end of the carriage mechanism.

The Lexikon is, in short, the kind of object for which it is possible to make allowances. To enjoy, without asking too

Below: Ettore Sottsass designed the Valentine typewriter, not as a writing machine, but, as he puts it, 'to keep poets company on Sunday afternoons in the country'

Right: The trouble with Mario Bellini's Lexikon typewriter, designed for Olivetti, was that although he got the looks right, he couldn't deal with the mechanics, so the machine becomes more and more unpleasant to use

many hard questions about what it is exactly that it does. Unfortunately, perhaps, for Olivetti, it seems that there are not too many people who are prepared to do that. Production of both the Valentine and the Lexikon has been abandoned.

Rather more successful, but in many ways attempting a similar task, is the Brionvega TS 505 radio, which comes from the same stable that produced the world's first black plastic cube portable television set. The radio was first launched in 1965, and was, like the Walkman, the product of a deliberate attempt to create an active, outdoor image for what had always been an indoor, static product. There were, it was true, tiny portable transistor radios around, but these had always been shoddy plastic products. Instead, Brionvega hired Marco Zanuso and Richard Sapper to take their new product in a different direction.

What the two of them came up with was a hinge. With magisterial authority, the radio is split in two halves. In one is the loudspeaker and the on-off switch. In the other are the tuning dial, volume control and an array of other switches and dials. The idea is that you open up the two halves to turn the thing on and find your station, with the two kept in place thanks to the help of a magnet set into the plastic. Then, with the station safely tuned, you snap the two halves shut again, flip up the built-in carrying handle, and set off on your stroll down the Via Montenapoleone, or Covent Garden's Neal Street, as the case may be. Of course, the thing wasn't ever really used like this at all. In every day use it sits on the polished glass desktops of the kind of people who shop at *Joseph Pour La Maison*, and who judge status in terms of street names – so much more subtle than in terms of manufacturers. Think about it, Knightsbridge, Rive Gauche, Park Avenue, all of them carry a bigger clout these days than Gucci, Bloomingdales, or Vuitton. It's all to do with making things more difficult for new arrivals. The rules keep being changed, though what's behind them stays the same.

In this kind of world, the Brionvega has all that it takes to become a domestic totem. There is its Euclidian symmetry and there are switches that not only give off a satisfying clunk as they move backwards and forwards, but suddenly show off a flash of bright red to show that they are on, and a vivid green when they are off. Brionvega have produced two versions of the radio. The first had a tuning dial with a chrome knob centred in the middle of one of the boxes, and was designed with the austere simplicity of one of those mantelpiece tombstone wirelesses of the 1930s. The present version which superseded it is more playful, with a heavily textured abstract pattern all over the loudspeaker, and an off-centre tuning knob.

The radio is fast becoming an anachronism, and turning it into a cult object of sorts is a matter of sheer survival for most manufacturers. Sony tried the trick with a neat little matt black shortwave model that is no bigger than a paperback, but which is crammed with a satisfying array of sliding tuners, textured keys, and maps of the world – handy if you are using yours to navigate solo round the world in a sailing boat but less so for finding the news.

In England, Roberts have managed to create a cult object out of their portable radio by the simple expedient of doing nothing at all to the design for thirty years. It still has a cloth covered wooden case, an archaic oval shaped dial, and a chromed loudspeaker grille. The effect is close to one of those half-timbered Morris estate cars, and it appeals to the same Fair Isle pullover crowd.

The only radio that really matches the authority of the Brionvega as a cult object is the Beolit 707, produced by the Danish firm of Bang and Olufsen. That number designation alone gives the game away. It is a product of the early 1960s, when jet travel was about to rule the world, with the honours being snatched by Boeing from the ill-fated Comet. It is a child of the era of midnight blue, drip-dry suits, of an age when the miniskirt was young, and jazz clubs were in their prime. A moment before we all got too self-conscious about things.

B & O escaped entirely from the oatmeal and open sandwich image of Denmark, and produced a machine with a much wider appeal. It is a Third Programme sort of radio all right, but one which still appeals to the BMW owner. The definitive version is in black, with a strange burnt charcoal texture to it. There is a matt black steel carrying handle and frame, and textured black panels on each side. At the top are the tuning controls, lettered in plain white sans serif, with a slide-rule affair to do the tuning. Instead of the conventional pointer to tell you which station you are on, there are a couple of magnetized ball-bearings. It's a deliberate attempt to produce a look that tells you it is all about precision, high quality and high performance.

The camera is an intriguing example of a product that must span the gap between two very different groups of users. That is the professionals, on the one hand, who see themselves as relying on no-nonsense precision-made technical instruments that must perform well in a crisis, but who in practice have all the same magpie instincts as all the rest of us. And, on the other hand, the amateurs, who merely wish to record their progress around holiday resorts, but will be unlikely to thank the manufacturer if they can do this only with machines that instantly spell 'amateur'. There are odd paradoxes, however, between these two clearly defined groups: Oskar Barnack, the designer of the Leica Camera in 1913, was the first to tackle the task of creating an easily portable high-quality camera which could be used by non-professionals with a

Right: Built like a Danish town
hall of particularly advanced
design, Bang and Olufsen's Beolit
707 radiates 1960s drip-dry
modernity from every pore of its
grainy plastic case to its very
name. With slide-rule tuning, it's
obvious that <u>what</u> it does is much
less important than <u>how</u> it's done

60

minimum of instruction. Yet it has now become identified with the most fanatic of professionals who wilfully revel in its consciously archaic lack of built-in devices.

Barnack's prototype did not see production for twelve years, when it finally emerged as the Model A Leica. It was a remarkable achievement, creating a form for a camera from scratch that was entirely free of any ornament or superfluous frills. The starting point was the 35 mm film format, which turned out to be the size of the future, along with such other, for its time, radical departures as a rangefinder.

The result was a camera that was far more practical to use than the monstrous plate cameras of its day, but which also produced more impressive results than the blurred snaps of the contemporary box Brownies and bellows-focus Kodaks. In the long run, of course, it was the unchanging shape of the Leica that made it a cult object. Its simple oval form has come to be identified with the uncompromising purity of design of the Bauhaus and the 1930s. In the end it became a byword for quality, attractive in a perverse way for its inconvenience. Long after the Japanese had taken over the 35 mm single lens reflex market with a vengeance, Leica was sticking to its original formula; this included a dogged refusal to include such newfangled notions as the built-in light meter, which resulted in the ritual of waving light meters

around at the target. Antediluvian, but it made people feel they were doing something that was worth the effort.

The Leica's pure shape obviously influenced the even more remarkable design of the Minox camera in 1937. The Minox was the first of a whole raft of James Bond accessories, serving as *the* spy camera. The film was stripped down 16 mm, contained in tiny spools, which allowed the rest of the camera to be scaled down accordingly. It was one of those designs shorn of the sell factor, no frills, no tricks, that instantly turns into the most potent of selling propositions. Well, not instantly. The Minox was produced by an outfit called VEF, operating out of Riga in Lithuania, which was not, perhaps, the best of marketplaces for a product like the Minox.

Walter Zapp's design with the smooth, rounded contours of a beach pebble, and an ingenious wind-on mechanism that combined the lens cap in a single push-in, push-out manoeuvre was merely biding its time until it reached the West after the war. It was the kind of thing that secret agents really did use in their safecracking, plan-copying activities. But it was also the inspiration for a range of other more instantly commercial products, like the Olympus XA camera. Now these are not miniature cameras in the sense that they use standard 35 mm film. But the Olympus is small and tough enough to drop into the pocket, and it has a sliding

Left and below: The Leica, on the market since 1925, was the first high quality camera to emerge from the hood and tripod era. Its shape has changed very little since. Original model, below, 1960s model, left. The company eschewed the technical refinements that would have made it easier to use, however it retains a remarkably silent shutter action which endears it to certain users

front mechanism that not only cocks the cam
but also protects the lens.

The Japanese also had one or two other
notions up their sleeves which have turned
the XA into a rather more viable
proposition: like the fact that the case is
made of plastic, which is cheaper and lighter
than metal; and the electronic built-in light
meter which controls exposure time. The
Olympus changed the ritual of photography
beyond recognition. Instead of being a
bright, shiny, look-at-me appliance that you
carry around on your neck, flaunting the
object – a process, incidentally, that has
been assisted in recent years by the
introduction of three-inch wide brightly
coloured straps bearing the maker's name –
the Olympus is the kind of camera which is
discreet and almost invisible. It offers its
owners more private pleasures than obvious
showoff display. There is the touch of its
rounded forms, the bright red piezo-electric
shutter that does away with the effort
needed to push down on a mechanical
shutter: you merely touch the red plate on
top of the camera, and you set the thing off.
An even more obvious addition to the play
value is the time-delay mechanism for the
shutter. Pull out a detachable lever arm on
the base of the camera, and press the
shutter and you have twenty-four seconds
to rush round in front of the camera and get
yourself in the picture. To let you know how
you are doing there is a red flashing light on

the camera that starts to emit a highly businesslike bleep, and quickens in pace after the first twenty seconds to give you a countdown; and that is accompanied by an even more frantic flash of the light built into the front of the viewfinder. No wonder people want to buy the thing. It somehow manages to flatter the hand that carries it.

Polaroid have also learnt the value of producing products that carry with them more than simpleminded utility. They have had to, ever since Edwin Land perfected his self-developing film and started the company in 1947. If his products were going to sell, they would have to do so in the teeth of bitter competition from the rival manufacturers, and in the absence of any other equipment suitable for taking Polaroid pictures but his own. The Polaroid strategy to deal with this has been to make the most of the process of taking pictures, to create cameras that are in themselves a pleasure to use. The example of the Polaroid range that has taken this approach to its most successful conclusion is the SX-70, developed at the same time as new high-quality colour polaroid film stock that did away with as much as possible of the wasteful paper and packaging that is an inevitable byproduct of the instant film process. The SX-70 is an elegant folding model that, in its carrying position, folds down into little more than the size of a paperback. The frame is burnished steel, with inset leatherette panels – signifying

class, in a manner that suggests qualities akin to those elements of uppercrust accoutrements that accompany shooting parties on to the grouse moors – hip flasks, folding binoculars and the rest. Lift open the top of the camera, and you are ready for action.

Taking pictures with the SX-70 is accompanied by a range of highly satisfying sounds – press the shutter and you get a very businesslike whoosh, as the camera's electric motor spits out the exposed film, ready for developing, and for you to take the next picture. The sound is so appealing that it's going to encourage you to fire off another couple of exposures, just for luck: all good for Polaroid's film sales.

There are some gadgets that, by their very ubiquity, have turned into something altogether more durable and significant. The telephone is certainly one: a machine that has turned itself from a novelty into a device which has completely altered the way we live. In Britain the Post Office monopoly on the telephone service helped ensure that there was one universal handset used throughout the country. And taking its responsibilities as seriously as the BBC under Lord Reith with his celebrated insistence on dinner jackets for announcers, the GPO's standard instrument for nearly thirty years was an object of such polished good taste and quiet excellence that it has set a standard that has never been bettered. It will certainly not be equalled in the

66

tawdry collection of gimmickry that is currently flooding the world's telephone shops.

The classic handset was designed by Jean Heiberg, and was made in its millions by Siemen's British subsidiary. Its suave, sharply delineated lines contrast effectively with the soft curvaceous forms of the earpieces. Made from Bakelite, and always either black or white, the telephone was one of the rituals of daily life with its drawer in the base containing a celluloid flap for keeping numbers. Its mellow bell, and even the named, rather than all-figure, telephone exchanges were all part of the experience. Telephones have become lighter and lighter. Freer, more florid shapes have been attempted, but none have been as well resolved, nor as quietly distinctive, as Heiberg's original. Using one now is an act of calculated anachronism. It suggests immediately the long-vanished world of Harris tweed, Mark 10 Jaguars and tennis club dances.

Gadgets are cult objects that maximize play value. They are the things that you put on your desk to cheer you up when the day is beginning to drag. They are there to tell the people around you what sort of a person it is they are dealing with. They have enough of a foot in the practicality camp – like the Rolodex, that superb piece of Americana from Seacaucus, NJ, with its chrome case and Bakelite Art Deco click-stop knobs to flip through your card index

in the most businesslike manner possible – to ensure that they are taken seriously. Cult objects cannot be entirely frivolous. They must also have those essential qualities of authority, presence, and the tactile qualities that make objects good to use and which give them a personality.

A useful indicator of a gadget's cult status is the extraordinary canonization represented by the magic words, 'selected for the permanent collection of the Museum of Modern Art'. A blessing with this ritual incantation is a far more valuable prize, for the product designer or manufacturer, than, for example, one of those odd little Design Council approved tags. And that's true even if their matt black calculators go out of production immediately afterwards, or their handcrafted toothpicks are manifestly non-functional.

MoMA is so over the top with its seriousness that its selections sometimes verge on self-parody. But there *is* a curious effectiveness about the idea of being able to buy a product, especially an everyday product, which is also to be found in a museum. It raises intriguing questions about how you treat such items. Are they to be kept in glass cases, to be preserved in their original condition, untouched, at carefully controlled conditions of temperature and humidity? When they include such mundane objects as black steel torches as hefty as a patrolman's nightstick, and household scissors, there is a faint but

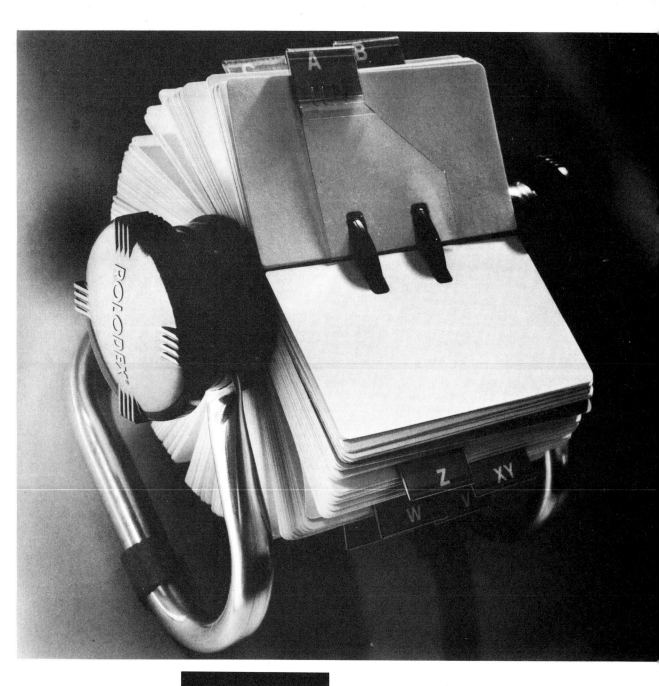

unmistakable aura about them. They hint, perhaps, at another way of life, one in which all objects are designed with the same glossy, slick purity that the Museum of Modern Art – for the past thirty years under the control of Arthur Drexler, New York's ayatollah of taste – has chosen to equate with the idea of being modern.

With calculated artlessness, Drexler calls Modernism nothing more than 'the simplification of form, and the creation of polished, highly finished surfaces'. And that holds good as far as Drexler is concerned for everything from skyscrapers, to the clocks, cutlery and furniture that he allows into his collection.

Displayed in all the splendour that the Museum can manage, bathed in dramatic pools of light, protected by Perspex, equipped with all the trappings of catalogue numbers, it is hardly surprising that Drexler's selections take on the status of a special category of object. Even when, like the Brionvega black box television or the Strathearn Audio turntable, they are no longer in production. Certainly Richard Sapper's Tantalo desk clock made by Artemide falls into this category.

Sapper's clock comes, inevitably, in black, or white, with a smoothly sculpted case that contains a conventional circular face within a sharply profiled and extremely slender evocation of the traditional form of the mantelpiece clock. Sapper has allowed himself more leeway with the graphics on the clock face, playing games with the spacing of the numbers and the way in which they are used. It is exactly the kind of clock you expect to be able to spot in the background of photographic spreads on smart new interiors in the pages of *Abitare* or *Domus* – although not, in all probability, of *Architectural Digest*. The sleekness and the shape are just the kind of thing guaranteed to make you want to pick it up and feel those oh-so-well-designed and polished curves.

It is the same with another of Drexler's choice items – Erik Magnussen's vacuum flask for the Danish firm of Stelton. The flask itself is the purest of pure shapes: a tall, slender cylinder, interrupted only by the most minimal of lips, and a black dot on each side that has something to do with the patent stopper device. With a shape like that, who cares what it does?

All those other gadgets have a similar purpose, the little black metal mesh ashtrays and filing trays, the propelling pencils in black metal, with a grip in black rubber, the Terraillon digital readout bathroom scales, the led thermometers, the designer staplers. The electrical goodies that we use at home are the same. The hifi turntables equipped with stroboscopic lights to monitor fluctuations in turntable speed, television sets equipped with clip-on stereophonic speakers, and studio monitor screens all make something special out of the most mundane of rituals.

Chapter Four

The importance of being Burberry

The language of clothes from Adidas to Zandra Rhodes. North of Watford in a Barbour, and how the West was won and lost in denim

Left: Old Burberries never die. A regiment of buttons drawn up in parade-ground order that hasn't changed since Lord Kitchener's day, across an endless expanse of cloth, tightly disciplined with an array of straps, buckles and belts

The trenchcoat has never been what you could call *dernier cri* fashion exactly. Thomas Burberry originally designed it, on lines suggested by his doctor, to be waterproof enough to keep the rain at bay, but still airy enough to refresh the parts that other mackintoshes could not reach, presumably with a view to cooling down any unwholesome passions aroused by that most potent of English aphrodisiacs, drizzle. It was a mild form of the rampant turn of the century mania for supposedly healthy garments, sparked off by Herr Jäger and his reform wardrobe. Jäger it was who reckoned that undergarments designed according to his principles could go six to eight weeks between laundering. Mr Burberry, at least, seems to have come to no harm from association with this quaint enthusiasm: he lived to be ninety-one, assisted perhaps by a lifelong devotion to militant teetotalism.

On the face of it, Burberry's formula was not one that was likely to attract the attention of the world's snappier dressers, but the British army, at least, caught on to the idea quickly. In the days when an officer and a gentleman had his uniform cut by his own tailor as a matter of course, and when prodigious feats of wrongheaded ingenuity were performed in the cause of perfecting the folding field armchair, the portable bath with built-in loofah, and the shell-proof humidor, a Burberry became as essential an accessory for the Boer War subaltern as a hip-flask and a Sam Browne belt. A chap could soldier on all day in one of Burberry's trenchcoats, secure in the knowledge that all those stout flaps and capacious vents would deal safely with the build-up of manly odours incurred during the course of one's exertions. The cloth, woven from the finest Egyptian cotton, was much lighter than that of any of its competitors. It kept the rain off, while allowing the body to breathe. All manner of ingenious details were devised to bring comfort to the man in the field. Pockets that kept their contents dry, sleeves that kept the rain out, even seams robust enough to make the garment serve as a makeshift bivouac tent.

The Burberry's arrival coincided with the switch from Imperial scarlet to khaki, which accounts for its colour. When the War Office gave the garment its official blessing in 1906, it set the seal on a new era of warfare almost as much as the tank and the invention of barbed wire. Yet the Burberry's generous cut and square shoulders still retained enough of the martial splendour of the past to smooth the traditionalists' transition into the age of utility.

During the Great War, the firm landed contracts to supply the military with sturdy waterproofs, and so, with a few refinements to the original design, was born one of the most pervasive cult objects of all, the definitive Burberry, better known, for obvious reasons, as the trenchcoat. More than 500,000 saw active service between 1914 and 1918. Thereafter, anybody who is anybody has at one time or another owned a trenchcoat. Bogart had one of course, so did Robert Mitchum. Lord Kitchener lived and died in one. Shackleton wore one on the way to the South Pole, Alcock flew the Atlantic in one – feats that Burberry's, always conscious of the value of good publicity, were not slow to capitalize upon. Spies, journalists and secret policemen inevitably have trenchcoats, if not always

under the name of Burberry. The Americans, in particular, adore them, producing their own copies, called things like London Fog which come equipped with lurid polyester linings, much to the indignation of Burberry's copyright lawyers.

There have been one or two changes made since 1914, notably a steady shortening of hemlines. Each season's cut is altered to take account of prevailing fashions, but today's trenchcoat is still essentially the same garment that our grandfathers went to war in. There is even a vestigial brass D ring on the belt, the ghost of the clip that the Tommies used to buckle on their cartridge boxes.

It is a remarkable tribute to the Burberry's longevity. Even Levis 501 red label jeans, whose origins go back still further into antiquity, cannot claim the same kind of continuity. Jeans have survived by transforming themselves from down home, honest-to-goodness farm wear, into the ubiquitous symbol first of youth in revolt, and then of the formerly youthful feeling their age. The Burberry, on the other hand, is still as respectable today as it was the day it was born. What's more it forms part of everyday life just as unobtrusively now as it did then, and there is precious little else that was in wide use in 1906 of which that can be said.

There have, of course, been some changes of emphasis along the way. Once an

Below: In the old days, Burberry was all about storm-lashed outdoor integrity. Now that wholesome image is being compromised by the spurious air of fumed oak clubmanship with which its showrooms are cluttered

elaborate, but unpretentious piece of specialized clothing, it became sought after, when the immediate horrors of the Great War had begun to fade, for the glamour it bestowed on its wearers from its association with the dangerous occupation of soldiering. For a while it also had connotations of the seasoned veteran, battered but unbowed – perhaps a little down at heel, but still proudly wearing part of the uniform in which he was demobilized.

After the Second World War, however, the trenchcoat's image moved away from specifically military associations, and towards all-purpose British nostalgia, in much the same way as tweed and Scotch whisky. Burberry themselves plugged this notion for all they were worth, opening up showrooms in places like Tokyo, New York and Paris that look like Laurel and Hardy's idea of a Pall Mall gentleman's club, all fumed oak, buttoned leather and heraldic crests painted on little plywood shields.

The key to the trenchcoat's attraction is its authenticity. It is an intimidatingly complicated sort of garment, studded with all manner of details that have become traps to catch the forger or the plagiarist. The genuine trenchcoat is beige, stone coloured, or field green, never black or navy, despite a regrettable tendency on Burberry's part to use these colours. It must have exactly the right number of buttons, dispositioned according to an immutable order of battle. Two stately rows of four march across the

chest. There are two more buttons under the collar, originally intended to hold a little triangular storm flap in place when required; this is still provided but is now on no account to be used. The flap at the back is secured with another button, and each pocket is battened down with one, or even two more. Both epaulettes are equipped with real buttons, not the cheapskate's corner-cutting device of a button sewn to the epaulette itself, making a grand total of at least 17.

The belt must be three inches wide, and is knotted, never buckled, or, a common error, tied at the back. Each sleeve has to be equipped with its own fully operational miniature belt, complete with leather covered buckle and fastening, relics of Mr Burberry's determination to stop wind and water from blowing up his customer's arms at tricky moments when they were taking aim with Gatling guns.

All this adds up to a very remarkable garment, pregnant with suggestion, and quite outside the bounds of what could reasonably be called fashion. But nor, strictly speaking, can it be described as merely utilitarian. The trenchcoat is a cult object, one of the fixed points of reference around which a language has been fashioned for clothes. Its shape and form have become classics of their kind, putting out identity signals so that initiates can recognize each other just as surely as masons exchanging curious little handshakes; even non-initiates have a chance of assuming a readymade

Below: 'During the War, I crashed in the Channel when wearing a Burberry and had to discard it. It was returned to me a week later, having been in the sea for five days. I have worn it ever since, and it is still going strong.' RAFC pilot officer, 1919

identity.

There is a cloud hanging over the Burberry, however, which even its legendary showerproof qualities may not in the long term be able to withstand. Precisely because the trenchcoat is such a ubiquitous object, Burberry are trying their best to give their product a unique identity, to set it apart from competitors imitating its style. They rely on an altogether unsubtle device of a tartan lining whose design they have patented, and now peddle vigorously a whole range of so-called accessories, that is to say tartan scarves, umbrellas, and luggage, with a relish that is altogether inappropriate for a garment that still aspires to quiet British understatement. Too much of this kind of thing, and the Burberry risks turning into a caricature of itself.

Not only are clothes intended to display wealth and status, but they are also tribal: they are there to give us a sense of belonging, or possibly even more important on some occasions, of not belonging. That is as true of the bespoke city type with turn-ups, and a detachable collar, as it is of the South London teenager in imported Italian sportswear that is far too expensive ever to risk on a playing field, but which does come in vivid easily identifiable colours. It is designed according to strict principles of legibility: the right number of stripes up each trouser leg; crests on polo shirts; and names on running shoes. The two groups may not have much else in common, but they are both using clothes to put across a particular message about themselves. And it is cult objects, such as the trenchcoat, which form the basis of the means by which that message is expressed. How you wear the particular object depends on what you are trying to say with it. At the height of the counter-culture boom of the 1960s, it was possible to find one or two aristocratic scions at Cambridge who appeared to be dressed in exactly the same neo-workman uniform of all their contemporaries, until one got close enough to discover that they had been slinking back to Savile Row to have their jeans and Donkey jackets specially made by the family tailor.

A similar kind of effect is being attempted, although rather less successfully, by those who use expensive materials such as suede, to look like cheap ones, such as bleached denim. This is vastly different from using cheap materials – usually the manmade ones – to look like expensive, natural ones, a course that is also to be avoided.

Different groups have different approaches to the question of what they wear, but all of them have their cult objects. The sober-suited stockbroker would die sooner than discuss the size of so much as a buttonhole with anyone but his tailor, or, in extremis, with the little man at Marks and Spencer who these days can offer a low-budget alternative that is almost as socially acceptable. Even with these confidants, conversation is as limited as it is with the sterner kind of barber, and confined to such issues as dressing to the left or the right, and the length of a cuff, rather than vulgar concerns of fashion.

The reluctance to discuss fashion can be explained by the sheer terror that most men have of buying clothes. They feel uncomfortable choosing anything more demanding than a shirt, and persuading them to remove their shoes, let alone their trousers, in a shop is a virtually impossible task. It is an unacknowledged feeling that also helps to explain the way in which clothes become cult objects. The whole fraught business is simplified enormously if instead of having to go to all the trouble and social anxiety of choosing a coat from scratch you can go into a shop and ask for a Burberry, or a pair of Levis, or whatever. Then all you have to worry about is the size, and not what the garment is going to be saying about you, because you already know.

From their earliest days at prep school, it has been instilled into every stockbroker, senior civil servant, cabinet minister and captain of industry just how important are the conventions of dress, the significance of the right type of buttons, the correct width of shirt stripes, and all the other messages imparted by the cult objects of his tribe. From the fourth former, allowed to unbutton his jacket but not to keep his hands in his pockets, to the prefect, granted the privilege of a flowered waistcoat, clothes are an inseparable part of caste and status, albeit one that is never put into words by those who subscribe to these particular values.

The average fashion-conscious South London teenager, on the other hand, is perfectly capable of sustaining a prolonged monologue based entirely on the names of the manufacturers of satisfactory garments. Once, a very long time ago, pullovers meant Pringle, and shirts were by Ben Sherman. Now it is more likely to be Armani that they have in their sights. Accordingly, Armani's social status has been undermined. From being the label favoured by the design world chic, it has come crashing down the scale, as the torrent of grubby tenners pouring into the coffers of London Armani retailers has swelled. It is a phenomenon, incidentally, which serves to underline the monotonous regularity with which history duly does repeat itself. Back in the earliest 1950s it was the West End tailors with respectable Savile Row premises who diffidently tried to interest their well-bred customers in a discreet Edwardian revival. Imagine their horror when they found that it was the Teds who fell upon those drape coats with delight, creating a deviant cult, accessorized by crêpe soles, bootlace ties and Elvis Presley jackets.

To become true cult objects, however, clothes have to have the stamina and the exposure to enter into the mainstream, if not to be worn universally, and then to be recognizable, at least at an unconscious level, to the majority of people. The longest lasting garments, like the trenchcoat and the Levis original jeans, do this with their shape, their material and the detail with which they are made.

It is also true that a simple name can be enough. It's the difference between the screaming headlines of tabloid journalism, and the nuances of the quality papers. The message that the use of the right manufacturer's name can convey is powerful, but it is not subtle. Well aware of this power, some manufacturers and designers have resorted to creating garments that are virtually all name. That is to say they are distinguished from countless competitors only by a label or crude identifying symbol. For the very insecure these garments provide the instant reassurance of a school uniform for the real world. A name emblazoned across a pullover, or etched on the buttons of a blazer confers both the anonymity of a uniform, and the prestige of identifying yourself as part of a wider group. So you've made a bit of money selling computer software and life insurance? You've moved up from the saloon bar to the wine bar and ditched the souped-up Escort with the clothes hanger in the back for a BMW. And you've twigged that Harry Fenton suits don't make it at the squash club. But how do you know what to buy instead? How can you be sure that you aren't going to be dropping clangers and spelling out exactly how far you have come every time you shoot a cuff or pull up your trousers before sitting down? No need to worry, the Dunhills and Lacostes, the Guccis and New Mans of this world are here to help. You can buy the complete works, the silk handkerchief in the right colours, the tie, the belt, the cufflinks, the shirt, the trousers, even the golf clothes. These guys must know what they're doing, they've got an address in Pall Mall, after all. The names are backed up with advertising, with shops that are designed to reassure the insecure that they are in good company, with packaging that increases your sense that here is an object of value. In short, a corporate identity is created. Customers are encouraged and flattered into feeling as if they belong to something. It is a technique used in the past by everybody from the Brownshirts to British Airways. Some firms employ a considerable degree of skill and subtlety to this end. Others anything but. Dunhill and Gucci use reasonably discreet typography, subdued colours and a soft sell. The sports people who have made fortunes from the curious habit of turning seemingly utilitarian pieces of equipment – running shoes, track suits and so on – into fashion, are anything but subtle. The Filas, the Tachinis and the Nikes produce garments that are midway between heraldry and advertising. Those names, those labels,

Right: Leaving aside the famous tasselled loafer for a moment, Gucci are quite capable of inscribing their initials on anything, from a pair of socks to a hold-all. It saves worrying about what you are saying with your clothes when the decisions have already been made for you

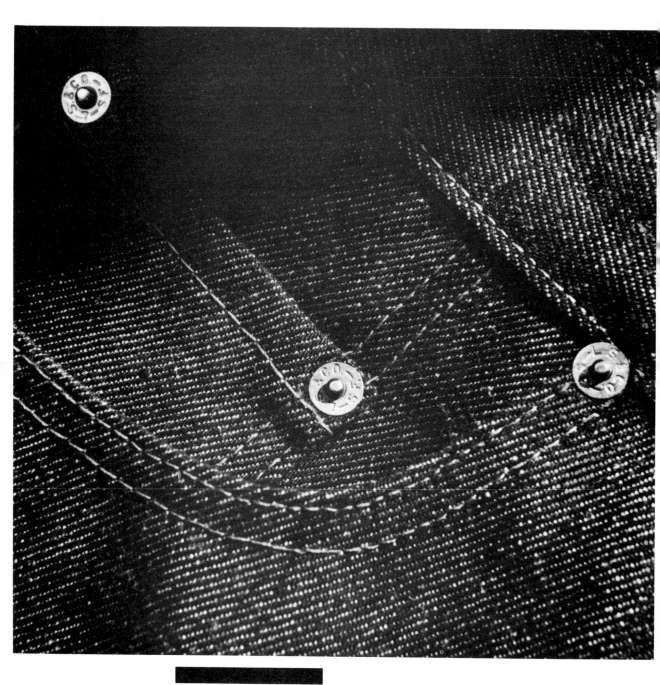

78

those styles, are the means by which you are able to spot at a glance, if not friends from foes – although it can come to that on the football terraces or the Bank Holiday beaches – then at least kindred spirits in a crowd. Hence the growing fad for celebrating the importance of a manufacturer's name by incorporating it using materials that are more precious or more durable than the garment itself: little metal tags, stitched to shirt and trouser pockets, for example.

In America, about as conformist a society, sartorially, as Albania, the clothes lines are drawn with ruthless precision. Dress codes are everywhere, and they mean business, which makes familiarity with the cult names and the cult objects vital for survival. For the young and upwardly mobile in Denver or Houston, and any of the other way stations on the ladder to corporate success, as much as in New York or Washington, nothing but Brooks Brothers will do. The brothers have grudgingly consented to provide suit cloth of different weights as a minor concession to America's extremes of climate. But a jacket of some kind must be worn, even in the most humid and ferocious of summers. And the strictures of the business dress code are as demanding for women as for men, including ties and pin-tucked collars for both sexes. Even when the yuppies are at play, their choice is just as severely limited: polo shirts and deck shoes are a compulsory part of the wardrobe. It is an American equivalent of the dowdiness affected by British young fogies in the interests of suggesting the security that comes from possession of large quantities of old money, but usually confirming exactly the opposite.

Any self-respecting subculture must develop itself a uniform in double-quick time if it is to be taken seriously in America. Hence the abiding infatuation of the homosexual community with lumberjack shirts and leather – more like fetishes than cult objects. Clothes put out a complex range of signs and signals. Some are obvious, while others are obscure to all but initiates. Who but the obsessed could distinguish between the rival attractions of Wrangler jeans, with a W stitched on to the back pocket, and the wavy V of the Levis trademark?

The gulf between Levis and the others is as wide and as mysterious as that which separates Coke from Pepsi. And yet there is no doubt that Levis are the real thing. The tidal wave of blue denim which drowned the world in a sea of bellbottom designer jeans in the 1960s and 1970s has at last subsided, leaving the original, the classic, the authentic Levis red tag 501, first made in 1850, as the undisputed master of the field. Herr Strauss, an emigrant tailor from Bavaria, first put his talents to work for the gold rush miners, making canvas wagon coverings for them. Jeans were a hardwearing sideline, aimed initially at the

Left: Levi Strauss perfected the classic 501 red tag jean in 1874 when he added copper rivets to the characteristic yellow stitching. Intended as utilitarian workwear, jeans make no bones about showing off how they are made. Now that they have moved up the social scale, the detailing is just a mannerism, capable of limitless manipulation – as demonstrated by everyone from Fiorucci to Gloria Vanderbilt

Right: Levis first made the jump from specialist workwear into the wardrobes of radical Hollywood types, playing at being working men the way that Marie Antoinette dressed up as a shepherdess. Real workers wouldn't be seen dead in jeans until they lost their 'work' connotations with the help of a thick layer of rhinestone in the 1970s

same market. The copper rivets were added in 1874 to protect the double-thread stitching at points of stress, according to the official story, or by some accounts, as a joke, played on a prospector whose friends had his jeans riveted by a blacksmith so that he'd be able to load up his pockets with rocks.

Genuine red tags are made of the heaviest weight of blue denim cloth, stiff enough to stand up by itself when new. The fly is concealed, and can be either buttoned, for traditionalists, or zipped. The cut is conservative, tight around the thigh, and even tighter about the legs, without actually tapering. The early usage of rolling up the bottom of the legs is now falling into disuse – Strauss was presumably offering only one size when he started.

Levis jeans are the first example of specialized work clothing jumping the social divide to appeal to those who, while they had no intention of doing so much as a day's physical labour personally, still wanted to use the toughness and self-evident practicality of denim to say something about themselves.

First on to the bandwagon were the Hollywood liberals, adopting the uniform of the workers to show (a) that their hearts were in the right place and (b) that they were secure enough about themselves to run the risk of wearing low status clothes, not that anybody was ever likely to take them as sharecroppers anyway. The more

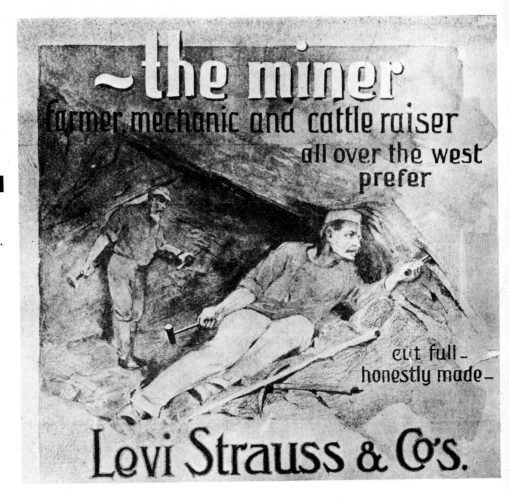

Right: Over the years, the Levi Strauss policy of advertizing heavily to create an identity for their wares hasn't changed much. The message, however, has

worn, patched and faded the fabric became, the more insistent the message. Only rich people can afford to be seen in old clothes. Poor people's clothes are too badly made to last long enough to look anything but new, and they are not likely to want to wear hardwearing work clothes, such as jeans, for any longer than they have to.

Blue jeans quickly became the universal symbol of white, middleclass kids, eager to show how little they cared about conventions. Some took the whole look to extremes, dressing from head to foot in denim, and going for voluminous dust bowl dungarees with huge brass buckles and denim work shirts. The effect was like the gilded Californian equivalent of Marie-Antoinette playing at shepherdesses. Today even Ronald Reagan wears jeans. Meanwhile, as the real proles became more affluent, no self-respecting member of the genuine working class wanted to be seen dead in denim, favouring instead polyester leisure suits and paisley patterned shirts. A curious inversion had taken place: a low status garment had turned into a high status one.

In Britain things were slightly different, with denim, initially at least, having connotations that were more to do with cowboys' fantasy and play than with work. But in America, it wasn't until rhinestone-studded designer jeans cut as tight as possible, with flamboyant insignia stitched across the pockets, that the descendant of Levi Strauss's once humble, working men's trousers began to retreat down the social scale, to become working man's wear again, a process that Tom Wolfe has skilfully chronicled.

While all this upstairs-downstairs hide and seek was going on in the West, over in Eastern Europe Levis had managed to turn themselves into the shorthand term for sex and drugs, rock music and decadence, a phenomenon which Eastern rulers were determined to resist, and their offspring were equally determined to share. All those unwilling recruits to the Pioneers in cardboard suits were prepared to do almost anything to get their hands on a pair of authentic Levis. The Soviet bloc initially resisted the blue denim invasion, but then, presumably worried at the hard currency draining away in the unquenchable thirst for jeans, they started signing manufacturing deals with the West to make their own.

As jeans began to be made in their millions everywhere from Hong Kong to Rumania, all sorts of liberties started to be taken with the original 501 red tag. Denim that was too light, or even patterned began to be used, and flares grew ever wider. And yet it was the red tag that remained the reason for the glamour of the whole species. The first jeans had represented such a departure in the way that clothes were made and worn that its repercussions are still being felt.

Strauss and his successors made a point of not wasting a great deal of superfluous fabric for display. Nor did he attempt to conceal the construction methods that he used, the double stitching and the pieces cut out of the fabric that go into a pair of Levis are clearly visible. Since jeans were intended for use on the prairie or in the garage, rather than the drawing-room, there was no reason to observe the niceties of the time which decreed that such details should be suppressed. But when Levis turned into fashionable garments, everything changed, and all these innovations were brought into polite society.

Perhaps the biggest precedent of all set by Levis was to use a label that not only showed off the maker's name, but did it in such a way that it became a permanent part of the garment after it had left the shop: a development that has since had barbarous consequences – it's not what you wear, but which name you have splashed across it that counts.

Levis also started the fad for distressed chic. Fresh from the shelf, they look absurdly baggy, and ooze indigo dye in quantities copious enough to turn you Ancient Britain blue. It is only when jeans start to shrink a bit, and when the colour begins to bleach that they really come into their own. In the 1970s, the attractions of worn denim led to the curious phenomenon of new garments being fashioned from recycled scraps of old jeans. And,

eventually, the process reached its wrongheaded extreme when brand new garments started being fed into industrial washing machines topped up with gravel, so that they would look battered and faded even before they reached the shop shelves. The same thing happened to the zippered leather flying jackets worn by the World War Two aces of the United States Army Air Corps. Like Levis, the whole point was to have one that looked battered enough to suggest that the owner was a veteran. The civilian copies made after the War to satisfy the growing hunger for this proto-cult object somehow weren't made of the right stuff. The smooth, shiny brown leather of the copies was all too obviously lacking that essential ingredient of battered authenticity. Lacking, that is, until some commercial genius hit on a process to age the leather artificially. Suddenly, anyone could buy themselves a war record off the peg; but, somehow, the charm went out of the whole image thereafter. It was all too easy: for it to work, you had to earn the faded look. It was the same with preshrunk jeans: the enthusiasts felt that they were missing something when they didn't have to suffer a cold bath in their new jeans to get them to shrink properly.

Levis and flying jackets were early examples of the way in which highly specialized clothes, intended originally for outdoor occupations – preferably dangerous ones, like parachuting – quickly become

84

fashionable. Jumpsuits, baseball shirts, carpenter's trousers, and even those American shirts that come emblazoned with the words Rudy's Diner across the back are all examples of this process. At first the secondhand versions sufficed to meet the demand from the cognoscenti. Later, copies that had never seen action started to be manufactured; they attempt to suggest the same indomitable qualities, usually losing much of the charm of the original in the process.

One item of military apparel that is rapidly gaining cult status is the U.S. Army drab olive field jacket, standard issue to all ranks, and equipped with a hefty zip, a built-in hood in the collar and Velcro fastened cuffs. It has already been through the war surplus phases and is currently being manufactured in several leisure versions.

The problem for those manufacturers who are still trying to appeal to the genuine specialists, who use their wares for the ends for which they were originally intended, is that they are compromised by the fashion image. The real professionals will switch to ever more obscure brands as they try to dissociate themselves from the amateurs. The process is at work not just with clothes, but with everything from sports equipment to hifi and even kitchenware.

The Barbour company is one of those firms that is having to fight exactly this problem, of combining popular recognition of the brand name, with retaining its credibility with the experts. The first John Barbour – it is still a family-run firm – went into business in 1890. He aimed his oilskins at people who needed them as working outfits: salt of the earth types such as fishermen, miners, farmers and gamekeepers. And the Solway Zipper, pride of the Barbour range, still has all the authority that comes from that pedigree, being both a highly specialized garment, designed for impressively rugged outdoor activities, and one that has the ability to grow old gracefully. The Barbour image, however, has been through some curious changes. From its humble but sturdy turn-of-the-century origins, when the company's first catalogue offered its Beacon Brand, 'absolutely water proof special light weight coat, popular for many years with officers of the merchant navy, post paid, 21/-', the Barbour came rapidly downmarket in the 1940s and 1950s with its association with the altogether rougher world of motorcycling.

In those days motorcycling was far from being the casual affair that easy to run electronic starter equipped Japanese machines have made it. Coaxing a monster like a Brough Superior or a Vincent Black Shadow into life was a Herculean task. And for the regular rider, oil was as much a constant companion as rain, and Swarfega an essential accessory. For these dedicated riders, the Barbour became virtually a

Left: The Barbour is perfect rural camouflage for townies. 'We belong' is the message. But before the Labrador set took to the Barbour en masse, it was the preserve of the Brylcreemed motorbike riders of the 1950s

uniform. For a start it looked as oily and grubby on the day that it left the shop as it would ever become. It also kept out the rain extremely efficiently. These bikers were not the tearaways in the sense that the California bikers of the same era were; they were more likely to be the members of the working class élite who couldn't afford a car, but were affluent enough to invest in an expensive bike to get to work on. And so it was that the Barbour came to have the same Brylcreem and bacon sandwich associations.

Things have changed again today. The Solway Zipper, better known simply as the Barbour jacket, is the instantly recognizable badge of the Range Rover and horsebox crowd, along with green Wellington boots – Uniroyal Hunters to be precise – navy blue Guernseys and brogues. Although the discreet advertising agency that Barbour employs to plug their wares in the most gentlemanly way possible calls its customers 'country people', the majority of its customers have a view of what constitutes rugged territory that is centred on Wimbledon Common. For these members of the Volvo owning classes, the utilitarian connotations of the Barbour are by no means unwelcome. They suggest a pleasingly democratic understanding between master and man, stalking game, or whatever else it is that honest rustics get up to, in the same sturdy and unpretentious outfits. The Barbour is above all an alibi, it's a working

outfit that says 'I belong here, I'm no rubberneck townie.'

Barbour's problem now is how to hang on to that businesslike image, and not get swamped by the popular fad for their wares. It is the fact that the Barbour is a real coat for real work that gives it its appeal. Barbour's self-promotion is accordingly low key. You can't shout about the kind of credentials it is trying to establish. Instead, Barbour tell you that it is the only company making thornproofs that has its 'finest long-staple Egyptian cotton specifically spun, woven, dyed and proofed for it in Britain'. The firm tells you about its solid brass press stud fastenings – which come with a corrosion proof oxydized finish, and a self-locating ball and socket mechanism.

There are legendary customers in the Barbour mythology who have survived zebra attacks, exposure to storm-swept, mid-ocean rocks and icy immersion in the South Atlantic, all thanks to their Barbours. And, in the company's South Shields headquarters, there are bundles of letters to prove that it all actually happened, even a letter from one man who lost his Barbour over the side of his boat on Lake Windermere, and eventually dredged it up again eight months later. After a good hosing to get rid of the mud and slime he sent it back to Barbour for reproofing, and it is now back in service. The Barbour range doesn't just stop at the Solway: they have everything from jockeys' jackets to

Below: The Solway Zipper, seen in-situ with a few other indispensable props for the rural way of life, a Rangerover and a Holland & Holland gun

Right: The green wellington boot, still one of the key passwords by which the English landed classes are able to recognize one another at long range. They perform equally well strategically positioned in the hallway as actually in action on the grouse moor

88

camouflage smocks on offer. But the heart of the range is their series of jackets which, in a charming survival of Edwardian practice, are all given a name of their own. There is the Border, lighter than the Solway, and the even lighter weight 28-ounce Durham.

There really was a Doctor Marten: and he was a German chiropodist. But the footwear to which he has given his name is vastly different in its connotations from the herbivorous and frumpy sandals manufactured under the name of Dr Scholl, which once also claimed the moral superiority of being designed according to correct anatomical principles. Marten invented a lightweight sole, in which layers of air were trapped in honeycombed moulded plastic. It was both tough, and comfortable to walk around in, being much more flexible than the heavyweight leather and nails alternative. His patent was adopted in Britain by the Northamptonshire bootmaker, R W Griggs, in the 1960s, and like many another cult object, the Air Wair boot that they produced began by appealing to a very narrow specialized group. Resistant to oil and acid, and with a ridge-profiled sole, the Air Wair was just the thing for fish-market porters working long hours on their feet in surroundings with very slippery floors. The eight-eyelet classic, available in cherry red or black in the original design, owes a lot to the look of the contemporary British Army issue boot,

although it is sleeker, tidier, and really does give you that feeling of walking on air that the manufacturers boast about. As somebody once said, 'Doctor Martens make people look as if they would spring right up again if you knocked them down.'

The skinheads were distinguishable by their close-cropped hair, their Crombie overcoats, pastel buttondown shirts, tight blotchily bleached jeans, and, of course, their boots. The look was derived from blue-collar America – early followers even had Sinatra-style snap brim trilbys. But the Dr Marten's – or DMs – were an entirely British, and deliberately intimidating, addition. The jeans were rolled up around the calves to reveal the DMs in all their cherry red glory. The eight-eyelet was the approved model, but a twelve-eyelet version was also acceptable, and really hard cases bought the monster version that reached almost as far as the knee.

The skinheads came and went, and came again. But they bequeathed their boots to a much wider audience: DMs were tamed and civilized. They provided a boot that felt good to walk around in, with which deliberately to spell out that you were not to be meddled with; and they were the exact opposite of soft and soggy suede desert boots, whose final demise Dr Marten's brought about.

Left: The meek and mild origins of the Airwair Bouncing Sole, designed by a German chiropodist, made its later transformation into an essential prop for the most menacing of the '60s youth cults all the more surprising

Chapter Five

The hot seats

What a room of your own will tell the world. Who put the poise in Anglepoise. How big is an executive desk, and what happens when everyone has a Cesca chair

Left: In furniture terms, designing a cantilever chair was the equivalent of splitting the atom. The race to produce the first successful version provoked a bitter series of law suits, but Marcel Breuer's version has lasted longest

The whole point of furniture, according to one more than usually jaundiced purveyor of outwardly modest and unassuming tables, chairs and sofas, is to help us to impress our friends. We are looking for convenient signposts with which to hint at how affluent, well-bred, up-to-date, discerning, or any combination of all four we are. Clothes do all that, too, but even the most flamboyant of dressers can only manage to don one outfit at a time. A whole house, on the other hand, offers enough scope to satisfy the ambitions of the most tireless of social mountaineers.

This is, of course, an approach fraught with dangers for the unwary. Inviting outsiders into the home is socially just about the most hazardous undertaking imaginable. It is hard enough to keep all those signals and messages by which we categorize and interpret each other under control on neutral ground. In the home it is virtually impossible. There is just too much going on

to keep track of. A home's contents volunteer so much raw information, and add up to such a complicated and personal message that they can't help but give too much away.

The lines are much more clearly drawn in the office. Everybody knows that office furniture is meant to map out status. It isn't just the question of how big and how expensive your desk is. Content is important, too. Big shiny electronic typewriters with daisy wheels and memories may be expensive, but they are certainly not the kind of thing an executive is supposed to have on his desk. Any manifestations of the tools of the trade must be strictly non-functional, limited to dried-up inkstands, for example. Nobody has quite managed to work out what to do about the desktop computer terminal yet, however. Keyboards are obviously low status, but there is a nagging feeling that the executive going places should at least be seen to be in

touch with all that raw computing power. In status terms, the likely outcome will probably be specially designed executive toy VDUs, parked in a drawer somewhere.

What is becoming increasingly clear to furniture designers agonizing over the implications of all this kind of thing is that furniture amounts to a language of its own. It has meanings and inflections that are subject to change over the course of time, just like any other language.

Using matching furniture throughout the house, so that every piece demonstrates a family resemblance, implies a tidy, nest-building mind, tinged with an acquisitive streak. Mixing modern furniture with a calculatedly chosen antique here and there is a device that works very much like the affectation of dropping French verbs into English sentences. Done with confidence it is a self-conscious demonstration of exotic erudition. But faltering over pronunciation signals, disastrously, exactly the opposite.

A couple of ancestor portraits deployed on the walls of a modest and very recently gentrified artisan's cottage are clearly intended to suggest an intimate familiarity with large country houses, claret and the great and the good; especially when they are combined with a sabre-legged silk upholstered dining chair or two. But in fact they are more likely to go behind their owner's backs once they are safely out of the room, and snigger to visitors at the boundless pretensions of their hosts.

With sledgehammer subtlety, overstuffed leather sofas the size of a sailing dinghy, for which whole herds of cattle have had to sacrifice their skins, are brought out in the hope of conveying the impression of sybaritic luxury and affluence, on a scale sumptuous even by Arabian standards. In the bedroom circular beds – mouthwatering confections whipped up from powder blue crushed velvet, and equipped with built-in video screens, and, demonstrating a suitable sense of bathos, an automatic teamaker – are an essential prop for feverish dreams of voluptuous suburban modernity.

Old money in America is suggested by means that vary in volume and vocabulary according to geographic location. On the East coast, or thereabouts, any item that aspires to high status, will be helped along by the designation, 'Colonial'. Fortunately for those who missed the *Mayflower*, the concept has apparently been stretched to include such previously undocumented items of the Pilgrim Fathers' luggage as built-in kitchen units.

Farther west, American tastes run to more flamboyant manifestations of heritage. Wall-mounted six-shooters, swinging saloon doors, and a whole panoply of buckskin fringed bric à brac are used to sort out the good guys from the recent arrivals. These goodies may look a little uneasy in such outposts of the new frontier as air-conditioned condominium towers in Fort Worth, but no more so than that remarkable

Left: The Barcelona chair (far right) is the nearest equivalent in furniture terms to the Gucci shoe. Costly to make and instantly recognizable, it is deployed in platoons in the reception areas of organizations around the world, in an attempt to signify probity combined with cultural awareness. It forms part of a family of Mies' designs which includes the Brno cantilever chair, and the Barcelona stool

hybrid of sartorial design, the Western business suit. Who could have imagined that the stetson would one day be transformed into an essential part of a formal wardrobe?

We use furniture in the hope of telling the world something that will rebound to our credit. But often we succeed only in putting across a message that is rather more accurate than we might wish. Small wonder then, in America at least, that the interior decorator has emerged as a crucial pivot of society. In the old days, elocution lessons and golf club membership were the passports to social acceptability for the newly wealthy. Now it is a spread in *Architectural Digest*. The stakes are too high to leave this kind of thing to the amateurs, hence the power and prestige of those decorators who can deliver the goods. The stars of the decorating business are quickly able to become fickle and costly tyrants, who must be pampered and flattered by their clients into working miracles for them.

Status, however, is only one part of the message that furniture can be used to convey. It is also there to reinforce the image that we have of ourselves, or, and even more important, the image that we would like the world to have of us. The romantic, yearning for the sun-drenched, leaf-dappled nostalgia of a non-existent rustic past will cherish the pine dresser, and the rush chair, as the perfect foil for baggy corduroys and sprigged muslin.

Those who aspire to evoke the Pimms swilling colonial era will resort to rattan. And people in search of an understated way of showing off their bank balance will choose the kind of chrome and black leather modern look – the indoor BMW approach.

Furniture can also aspire to the status of art. The Italians, in particular, are good at turning out the kind of stuff that hints none too gently that it is a species of cultural endeavour, rather than vulgar commerce.

These are all approaches in which furniture can assume a role as a cult object. For each one, there are a select number of pieces of furniture that exert an attraction out of all proportion to their ostensible role in keeping people's bottoms at the requisite height above the ground. These are the cult objects, the chairs, the tables and lights which stand out, not so much from considerations of comfort and utility, but because of their knack of putting across a whole look or style.

Furniture has only recently made the leap from being the product of master craftsmen, whittling away at pieces of wood with well-honed chisels, to the end-product of factories and conveyor belts. It is this change that has made it possible for some pieces of furniture to become cult objects. You can't, after all, create a cult from a one-off – there wouldn't be enough to go around.

Mass-produced furniture first appeared during the last century with Michel Thonet, one-time cabinetmaker to the Imperial

Right: Made in its millions, Thonet's basic café chair turned furniture from a craft into an industry, thanks to his patent steam wood-torturing process. Instead of being made in workshops, chairs were built on production lines, and a single design could turn up all over the world

Austro-Hungarian court. Thonet patented a technique to torture wood into sinuous curves by clamping it into metal presses while blasting it with hot steam. Armed with this lethal secret weapon, Thonet was able to turn out bentwood café chairs in their millions, as well as Art Nouveau rockers of baroque complexity.

Thonet's earliest café chair – known, somewhat laconically, as the B-27 – clearly qualifies as a cult object. So does the squared-off version, at least among the proprietors of nouvelle cuisine restaurants where raw liver and strawberries are considered an amusing combination. According to legend, it was produced as the result of a visit by Le Corbusier to the Thonet factory. 'How do you like our chairs?' they asked the master. 'Just fine, but they'd be even better if you did this,' said Corb. And he handed over a back of the envelope sketch.

At about the same time, the tubular steel cantilever chair, designed by Hungarian-born American architect Marcel Breuer, was setting off on a course to become the first purely twentieth-century piece of furniture to acquire cult status. At the absurdly precocious age of 24, Breuer was running the Bauhaus furniture design school. In one of those Newton and the Apple flashes of the blindingly obvious, Breuer was smitten, while out riding on his brand-new Adler bicycle, with the potential of tubular steel as a material from which to fashion modern furniture. If tubular steel was strong, supple, and light enough to support him in comfort while pedalling around the streets of Dessau why shouldn't it be equally handy for making furniture with, he reasoned.

Breuer's immediate reaction was to telegraph Adler's directors, urging them to branch out into furniture manufacture. Faced with a predictably chilly response, Breuer was obliged to take up his own challenge. He laid in a stock of tubular steel, and enlisted the aid of a plumber – who better to help unravel the complexities of welding one pipe to another? The result of this unlikely collaboration was the Wassily chair (Kandinsky was a friend of Breuer's). There is something not quite right about the chair from a design point of view. The frame looks too frantic and too busy for comfort, and its shape owes more to the handlebars of Breuer's trusty Adler than is good for it. Breuer was serious about producing a twentieth-century chair, however, and, with its interlocking stretched leather seat, back and arm rests, the Wassily was certainly quite different from anything that had gone before.

Breuer wanted to design a chair that you could build on a production line, just like a Model T Ford. But for the first thirty years or so of its life, the Wassily remained an obstinately handmade item, produced in workshops, not factories. The same was true of Breuer's most celebrated and

Right: Riding his Adler cycle around the Bauhaus, Marcel Breuer hit on the idea of tubular steel furniture. Clearly it was the handlebars of his machine that made the most lasting impression

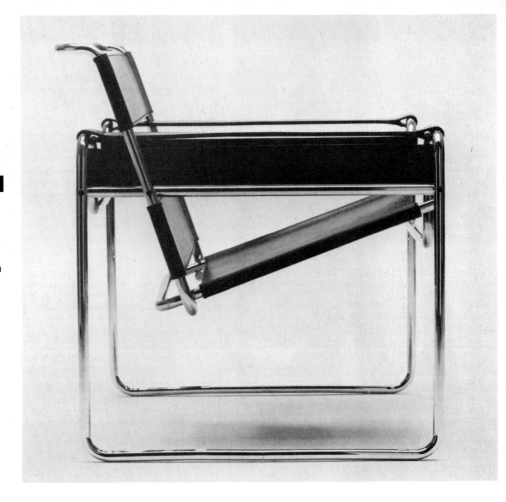

98

successful design, the tubular steel cantilever chair that he designed in 1928 called the Cesca chair after his daughter Francesca. In the 1950s and '60s, however, Breuer's design began to be copied all over the world. Though the Cesca was made in ever increasing numbers, it didn't do his royalty cheques much good, since the authorized version cost ten times as much as the pirated chair, and was to the casual observer, at least, indistinguishable. But it did ensure that the chair became what Breuer had always wanted it to be: an economical and practical piece of everyday furniture. Depending on the context in which it is used, the Cesca today can still flaunt its avant garde origins, yet it can also blend unobtrusively and equally successfully into the background.

Breuer was not the first person to come up with a cantilever chair – in furniture design terms, the equivalent of splitting the atom. Mart Stam, a truculent Dutch contemporary narrowly beat him to it, and Mies van der Rohe wasn't far behind him with a version of his own. But both had seen Breuer's first experiments with bending steel tube, and there are suspicions that Breuer had told them both that he was working on a cantilever chair. The cantilever would pull off the ultimate 'look, no hands' trick, appearing to be supported by two legs, rather than the customary four.

Stam won the patent race, sparking off a whole series of lawsuits alleging plagiarism

and piracy against his rivals throughout the 1930s. These got so bitter that Breuer eventually took himself off to Britain in disgust, and subsequently to America, where he gave up furniture altogether and returned to his first love, architecture. Designing a cantilevered chair is not just a question of getting the balance right between the legs and the back. You have to find a way of fitting in the seat and back rest too. Stam opted for leather, stitched directly around the steelwork. Mies, as one might expect from a man dedicated to doing more with less, designed a simple S-shaped chair with a basket-weave seat. Breuer went for the cheaper option of putting in a separate wooden frame that could support a fragile cane seat. It was Breuer's solution that turned out to be the most economical in the long run, and it was Breuer who ushered in an era, characterized by the architect Peter Smithson, when the ultimate test of design genius was your ability to produce a successful chair.

Most of architecture's first division tried its hand at chairs during the 1920s, possibly because they were starved of the chance of putting up any buildings. The results were often closer to miniature architecture than furniture design. You cannot possibly sit in Gerrit Rietveld's red blue chair, for example, and be under the impression that this is just any old seat. You can't help noticing that you are in the presence of art with a capital A, especially when you bark the back of your shins if you try to get up too quickly while overcome with admiration at Rietveld's masterly handling of intersecting planes. Curiously enough, Rietveld was originally under the impression that he was producing a low-budget chair that could be knocked up by any jobbing carpenter equipped with a set of his easy-to-follow drawings. But somehow things didn't work out that way; and any attempts to do so now will end up in legal threats from the heirs to Rietveld's patents. The chair has turned out to be a member of that curious class of objects in which the ostensible function is reduced to a purely symbolic part of the design. It is a phenomenon not unlike the custom among army officers of carrying swords on ceremonial occasions. A new purpose has overtaken the original one; that of saying something about the status or proclivities of its owner.

Chairs have evolved extremely specific meanings that are not always related very closely to what their creators originally had in mind. Mies van der Rohe's Barcelona chair, for example, began life as a throne for the King of Spain, designed for his use at the opening of the German Pavilion of the Spanish World's Fair at Barcelona in 1929. Since then it has turned into *the* chair to be stationed in pairs at the reception area of companies wishing to signify probity, prestige and cultural awareness, tempered with conservatism. Property developers, large banks, and the older kind of airline all love them. They are particularly popular in the Third World, where they have become as much a part of the essential trappings of national pride as a fleet of Mercedes, a steelworks and a clapped-out old Boeing masquerading as a national airline. An advertising agency of the more progressive kind would not be seen dead with even one of them, still less a pair. They prefer to opt for something a little more up to date, probably one of those liquorice allsort coloured Italian numbers that look like recycled bits of 1959 milk bars – 'look at our street credibility' is the message. Neither variety of such chairs is actually intended to be sat in – it takes the sheen off the leather. They are there as signposts. People don't actually want to sit in them any way. But being ushered into a reception chair is an essential part of the ritual that accompanies corporate visiting, as much as other non-functional rituals, such as the offer of a cup of coffee and the exchange of business cards.

Like Mies van der Rohe, Le Corbusier, working with Charlotte Perriand, dashed off a series of furniture designs at an early stage in his career, and then never returned to them. He, too, favoured black leather and chrome, and certain of his designs, the Grand Confort in particular, have the same role, signifying corporate probity, as the Mies chair, if not more so.

Le Corbusier claimed that his chaise longue – equipped with enough straps and studs to satisfy the most energetic and

Right: Buying a Le Corbusier
Grand Confort in architectural
circles is like acquiring a car
phone for a rising tycoon. It's
there to tell the world that you
have made it at last

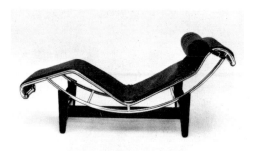

determined of fetishists – was inspired by watching too many Westerns. The villain is always discovered lounging on the porch of the saloon at some point, seated on a tipped up stool, his feet up above his head on the hitching rail, enjoying a cheroot. Le Corbusier set out to create the same effect, splitting the chaise into two parts: a low steel base and a movable superstructure that looks not unlike a toboggan with chrome runners. It allows the chair to assume anything from a prostrate dental consulting room back-on-the-floor mode, to an almost upright conventional sitting position. Unlike most cult items of furniture, this one is comfortable. And as its popularity has grown, so it has started to be manufactured in larger numbers – both in the form of faithful academic reproductions of the original 1928 design, and in cheaper knock-offs. Piracy is an entrenched part of the furniture business.

By definition some cults appeal only to the very particular needs and special interests of minority groups. In America, as Tom Wolfe was the first to point out, the Lay-Zee-Boy Lounger has been taken to the bosom of the Archie Bunker classes. This bloated shag-pile upholstered electrically operated rocking chair spells out the good life, spilling comfort and opulence in all directions for the master of the household, parked with all the grace of a Buick station wagon in front of his television set.

Then there are the design buffs, who are never happy without a Tizio light somewhere in the house. The Tizio, for the uninitiated, is the extraordinary looking table lamp – a kind of high tech Anglepoise fashioned from matt black steel, its joints picked out in red – which perches on desks and drawing boards with all the gawky, angular presence of a nesting stork. Sapper advances all kinds of strictly logical justifications for the design: that is to say, its weighted base and complex counterbalanced arms give it the maximum of stability with the minimum of encroachment on the working surface of a desk. But there is rather more to its attraction than that. You don't have to ask what your host does for a living if you find one in his or her study. You know that there is an architect around here somewhere. Then there is its streamlined look, the neat way in which you can bring the quartz halogen light to within inches of

103

104

the table top, oozing graph paper.

Interestingly, the Tizio is showing signs of breaking out of the design ghetto into the mainstream. After a walk-on appearance as a prop for a mad scientist type in one of the Bond films, the Tizio has started to be deployed in ever larger numbers. One cosmetics firm, for example, uses it at all its department store counters, almost as a signpost. Backing up its graph paper trademark, the Tizio is meant to show that this is a no-nonsense, highly scientific approach to keeping the wrinkles off the modern woman. Of course, the light it gives is highly flattering, too.

One lamp that has long enjoyed cult status is the original Anglepoise. Designed by George Carwardine in 1934, it has been in production in a form that has hardly changed ever since. Carwardine was looking for a convenient and practical adjustable lamp to help examine patients in the consulting room. He was tired of troublesome clamps and mechanisms that were too stiff to move with fingertip pressure. So he took as his model the human arm. In the elbow, muscles push and pull bones back and forward by acting in tension against each other. Using the same principle, Carwardine created a jointed light with opposed springs connected to the arms of the Anglepoise. (Horstmann based a tank suspension system on the same idea.) The heavy base keeps the lamp stable, and the lamp itself is contained in a fluted trumpet, which looks exactly what it is: a

no-frills means of delivering concentrated light to a specific point, without creating any dazzle. The whole thing has the looks that one would expect from a doctor: design shorn of superfluous styling tricks. It could be a standard piece of consulting-room equipment, as dour and unpretentious as a stethoscope.

Carwardine took his invention to Herbert Terry & Sons Ltd, a Midlands engineering firm more used to manufacturing springs than consumer products like table lamps. Despite this unpromising start, or perhaps because of the added air of authenticity that it bestowed on the Anglepoise, the light quickly moved beyond the highly specialized market envisaged for it. Its puritanical hair-shirt design appealed to the prewar Left Book Club Hampstead worthies who took to it with the same enthusiasm they had for those newly issued orange-spined Penguin paperbacks which they would read by the light of an Anglepoise, seated comfortably in their Marcel Breuer designed plywood chaises longues. Virtually unchanged for three decades, the Anglepoise spread far and wide, spanning the gap between lights that functioned as furniture, and lights treated as specialized equipment. The earliest version still looks as sturdy and dependable as ever, with its simple geometry, a stepped pyramid for a base, and a hemispherical shade. In the 1960s variations were introduced to the original design. A drawing-board version was

Left: With a design based on the workings of the human arm, the Anglepoise was first produced in 1934. Its simplicity and performance may have been equalled, but never bettered

brought out with a clamp replacing the normal base. The shade became lighter and larger, and the wiring was tidied away into the bones of the light, rather than being left dangling. Up to this date the Anglepoise's development as a cult object had progressed steadily. The changes in shape and style preserved the original character and quality intact. At the end of the 1970s, however, disaster struck. Terrys produced a lamp whose only relationship to the real Anglepoise was its name: a gawky, clumsy creation, completely lacking the swan-necked grace, and the convenience of the original. Gratifyingly, it was a commercial flop, opening the way one hopes to the reproduction of the 1934 original, a design of such authority and presence that it has become a genuine classic.

The trouble for the true cult aficionado of the Corbusier designs, the Anglepoises and the Tizios is that they have become too recognizable. Are they there just because someone is trying to tell you something? Choosing them becomes too easy, hence the hunt for ever more obscure designs with which to put across that extra edge that comes from being the first one to try something new.

The real designer's designer by that criterion is Eileen Gray, a remarkable woman who did her best work in the 1920s and 1930s, but never really earned the recognition that her talents deserved until the end of her very long life. When she designed her furniture, it was never produced in more than a few dozen copies. Now that she has become a cult figure, and so have her designs, her furniture is beginning to be produced in substantial quantities for the first time.

In some cases there was nothing much more for the manufacturers to go on than contemporary photographs of the originals. The extraordinary Bibendum chair, for example – which not only sounds, but looks exactly like its Michelin man namesake – had no surviving drawings left when Zeev Aram acquired the rights to manufacture it in the late 1970s. With the help of Gray's memory, and an advertisement in the papers appealing for pictures, or better still a surviving example, a faithful replica is now available.

Gray's furniture has the glossy chrome and black leather feel of Le Corbusier and Breuer, only more so. If you really want to lay claims to being regarded as a person of taste and discrimination, hers is the furniture to have lying casually about the place. Interestingly enough, it was also Gray who adopted the self-conscious device of giving her design a number, not a name. There is something quintessentially cultish about the idea. It smacks of a catalogue, of the engineer knowing what he is doing, ordering products shorn of the frippery of names. The practice has since been taken up by everybody from perfume manufacturers – Chanel, of course, to Levi

Right: Still for dedicated cultists only, Eileen Gray's chair, named, after the Michelin man, the Bibendum. Wider recognition cannot be much longer in coming

Strauss and their 501 jeans.

Hans Coray was the man who made perforated metal synonymous with high tech long before the word had ever been invented. Coray designed the Landi chair for the Zurich Fair of 1938, as an outdoor, stackable chair to be used in parks. It was high tech in both senses of the word. Up until then, aluminium had been confined to aeroplane wings. The chair is a one piece shell stamped out of a mould. The perforated holes are there partly to make it more rigid, and partly to let the rain run through. Take the thing indoors, and you have the whole high tech business, of course: using a park chair in domestic surroundings, raw metal and all.

Few chairs achieved cult status so quickly as Charles Eames's swivelling lounger and ottoman designed in 1956. Eames produced a chair that spelt good design just as unmistakably as it spelt luxury, a winning formula if ever there was one. All that business about mixing plywood and steel and free flowing curves had the design buffs queuing up. But even to people who found the prim, thin-lipped postwar Scandinavian good taste world, peddled by the hectoring do-gooders of the Design Council, a bore, the Eames lounge chair looked like the kind of thing you could get to grips with. For a start, while it didn't shout about it, it was clearly expensive: black, welted leather, and a sensuous rosewood frame saw to that; then there was the deep-buttoned back, and

the equally opulent stool to go with it – obvious comfort signals in any language. Most of all there was the masterful way that the thing could swivel round. This was the command post from which the master could keep control of his home, in comfort, but in undisputed sway over all he surveyed. Small wonder, then, that though the chair was made by a firm that specialized in office equipment, Herman Miller, or Miller as they prefer to call themselves, were able to start selling the thing in huge numbers to the new frontier America that was discovering the return of Camelot with JFK, and the joys of the Boeing 707.

The key thing about furniture cult objects is the way in which they are used. In practice, that is a matter of where they are positioned. Gather too many together in a single space and you end up with a museum. They have to work in conjunction with each other, and with their surroundings. Too large a piece for a particular room will look intimidatingly large – which may be a large part of the point. A pair of matching chairs, rather than just one, is sometimes needed for an object to come across with full force. Cult objects often need enough space to enable them to be seen from an angle. All this is the grammar of the language expressed by furniture. It allows the language to be used fluently and smoothly if followed.

Left: Designed in 1956, Charles Eames' black leather and rosewood lounger has been the acceptable face of overstuffed comfort ever since. It puts across a message of taste mixed with status in a gratifying combination for its owners

Below: There is an argument that Hans Coray invented high tech when he came up with this chair for the Swiss parks service in 1938. Not only was it made of perforated metal, but in the long run it turned out to be far more popular indoors

Chapter IX

Putting pack art onto the shelves

Never mind the price, look at the pack. How Coca-Cola made the world free for democracy, and Castro kept up appearances, while cigarettes dressed to kill

Left: Revolutionary fervour in Havana has never extended as far as the state packaging design department. Cuban cigars still enjoy all the crusty elaboration of the Edwardian typographer's art. Without it, the flavour just wouldn't be the same

There is a class of cult objects that depend for their particular charms on the skill – some puritans would call it the cunning – with which they are packaged. Their identity in other words, comes from the flair with which they are turned out; their character is formed by manipulating the consumer. Particular materials, shapes, typefaces and even names can all be used to signal a particular kind of product.

The special properties that make the smoking of a Havana cigar the twentieth-century equivalent of offering up a celebratory sacrificial lamb, for example, have as much to do with the splendid elaboration of the packaging, as with the dubious pleasure of placing a tightly rolled bundle of tobacco leaves in your mouth, and setting fire to one end. Even if you don't like the taste, it's impossible not to recognize that a cigar is something special. Despite the revolution, the Cubans have very wisely refused to tamper with the

traditional capitalist trappings of the cigar industry, for the export market at least. (There is, it is true, one brand of cigarillos named after Che Guevara which comes in a box tastefully decorated with a portrait of the counter-cultural Sixties hero worked in little tobacco leaves, but that comes from Italy.)

In Cuba itself, neo-colonialist plantation owners may or may not have ground the faces of the peons into the dust, but their names still live on in Fidel's workers' paradise, etched into the packaging that they had created for their wares with all the ostentation that their turn-of-the-century typographers could muster. The Number One State Tobacco Farm does not have quite the same ring about it.

Just think about all the layers that you have to get through before you have a chance to light up a cigar. These are products so precious that they must be kept in humidity controlled vaults. Inside the

humidor, those colourful wooden boxes, decorated as gaudily as an ambassador's state uniform and sealed with documents that look as solemn as a blue chip share certificate, are piled up with all the loving care of bars of bullion. Once you breach that barrier, you find enough tissue paper inside the box to stock an entire counter at the average Comecon department store, along with slivers of wood to separate the ranks of cigars from each other. There may even be an individual aluminium torpedo tube as a further protective screen, followed by the pièce de résistance, the band around the cigar itself. Etiquette on the disposal of this last varies according to circumstances. But on the whole it is considered more robust to smoke with the band still in place, rather than to risk damaging the fragile wrapper leaf of the cigar with too vigorous a removal.

Throughout this three-act performance, a sense of quality and connoisseurship has been steadily built up from the expectations established by the teasingly slow process of discarding layer after layer of packaging. This, and not plain raw cost, is what makes a cigar a luxury, and a ritual not just a product. As the designer Wally Olins puts it in his treatise on corporate identity, 'A Montecristo just wouldn't be the same shrink-wrapped and displayed in a sachet dispenser next to the Wrigleys Chewing Gum and the Benson and Hedges cigarettes.'

Does all this mean that it is the package, rather than its contents, which constitutes the cult object? It is a moot point. Certainly if the contents of a package manifestly fail to live up to the expectations that the packaging has aroused, then the authority of the pack and the message of its style is rapidly undermined. If, after all that business with humidors, boxes, tubes and bands, you find you have been fobbed off with some inferior Jamaican leaf, then no amount of gilded wrapping will be any consolation. On the other hand, so strong is the identity of some packs that they retain their power even when empty. And, in many cases, it is the package itself that has played the major role in establishing a market for the product.

Certainly Coca-Cola would be just another heavily promoted tooth-rotting fizzy drink without that bottle and the famous florid script. And this is a fact of which the Coca-Cola Corporation is very well aware. Despite the advent of the can, and even more character-eroding developments, such as the invention of the standard two-litre polycarbonate bottle, Coca-Cola has kept its archaic recyclable bottle alive. It is one of the most potent cult objects of all time, collected with obsessional devotion, the subject of paintings and studies, and shorthand for a whole way of American life, albeit one that is now under increasing threat in these diet and health conscious days.

Coca-Cola was born in the days of snake

Left: First bottled in 1886, the buxom curves of the Coke bottle have made Coca-Cola not just a fizzy drink – 'esteemed brain tonic' as it was called in its early days – but a universal symbol of Americana. Even though cans and plastic now account for the vast majority of sales, the classic post-1955 bottle is still kept alive for image-building purposes

Below: The original Coke bottle as used from 1915 until 1955 when Raymond Loewy slenderized it

131

oil, quack medicine and hucksters peddling patent remedies at travelling fairs. Originally a lethal-sounding cocktail of cocaine, sugar and nut oil, it was perfected in May 1886 by one Dr John S. Pemberton, a chemist from Atlanta, and named by his business associate, Frank Robinson. In the beginning it was an over-the-counter elixir, peddled as 'brain tonic', before going straight as a beverage available in a coloured glass medicine bottle, and finally, purged of the cocaine, into a much imitated soft drink. Of its earliest rivals, only Pepsi-Cola has survived the attentions of the patent and trademark lawyers. It, too, was the product of a southern chemist, who aimed at the stomach rather than the brain. He claimed his formula was a cure for indigestion, putting the pepsi in dyspepsia. The process of turning a so-called medicine into a soft drink can still be seen at work with products like Lucozade, until very recently packaged in orange cellophane to give a spuriously medicinal look.

During World War Two, Coca-Cola pledged itself to providing limitless supplies of the drink that things went better with for every American fighting man wherever he was in the world at just the same price he paid for it back home, a boast that was achieved thanks to a network of frontline bottling plants. It was these that formed the basis for the ubiquitous postwar Coke. The bottle, as everybody knows, began to appear with Japanese, Chinese, Arabic, Hebrew and even Cyrillic versions of the logo.

But, somehow, Coke never took on the air of hands-across-the-sea internationalism that its American proprietors tirelessly worked toward. Coke is synonymous with the boundless ambitions of American business, and with the way in which the whole world is willing to adapt its tastes towards those of the great American dream. The Coke ads might feature a diplomatic ethnic balance, but there was no mistaking it, Coke was Uncle Sam's favourite tipple, and he didn't mind asking for it in Maxim's if he felt like it. The bottle itself, from its origins as a sombre medicinal flask, has been through several incarnations, from its prim neolithic phase, to the fullblooded Mae West curves of the 1920s. Even Raymond Loewy, the indefatigable former fashion illustrator and self-publicist, with a self-appointed mission to redesign America, as he put it, and who claims the credit for everything from the space shuttle to the Greyhound bus, has had a hand in shaping the Coke bottle. It was he who Coke called in to slenderize curves judged too buxom for the modern world in 1955.

The ubiquitous Loewy was also responsible for the Lucky Strike cigarette packet, as all-American a cult object as you could hope to find, and one which is even worse for your health than Coke. The Lucky Strike pack is a throwback to the pre-crushproof box era, when cigarettes came in paper packs, or cups as they were known,

Right: Even when it's empty, the Lucky Strike packet has something about it. There must be strong magic about anything that is so ubiquitous in America

Right: The French enthusiasm for all things modern and transatlantic even extends to cigarettes. The Disque Bleu packet clearly owes a lot to Loewy's Lucky Strike pack

and when their contents were transferred to gentlemen's cigarette cases. But a Lucky – 'it's toasted' – was the working man's cigarette, and it stayed in the paper pack. The pack could be slipped into the chinstrap of a GI helmet, or twisted into the cap-sleeved teeshirts of walkers on the wild side.

Unsurprisingly, the name, first used in the 1850s, was coined at the time of the gold rush. American Tobacco produced Lucky Strike cigarettes for the first time in 1917, in the far-off days before the Surgeon-General of the United States had determined that cigarette smoking was hazardous to your health. The pack is, and was, a masterpiece of simplicity, so nonchalant in its typographic naïvety that it beats the spots off the most sophisticated and artful of graphic designers. For 1917 it was a model of positively Bauhausian purity – a red disc on a green ground, with a plain sans serif typeface spelling out the name across a bull's eye. Loewy, never a man to nurse an inferiority complex, tells the story of his involvement with the pack like this: 'In March 1940, George Washington Hill, no less, walked into my office unannounced and said, "You Raymond Loewy?" I said, "Yes, I'm Raymond Loewy." He then took off his jacket, kept his fishing hat on, sat down, and threw a pack of Lucky Strike on my desk.

'"I'm from American Tobacco." (He was the president.) "Someone told me that you could design a better pack, and I don't believe it." "Then why are you here?" I asked. He looked at me for a moment, grinned, and we were friends.

'Without further ceremony, he pulled an attractive cigarette case out of his pocket. "Cartier," he said. "Only the French can make these, and look at these suspenders. Cartier too." "So are these," I said, showing my own, which Cartier had made for me.

'"Well," he said, "what about that package? Do you really believe you could improve it?" "I bet I could," I answered.

'We bet fifty thousand dollars. He left, and in April the new Lucky Strike pack was adopted with resulting large sales increases, creating, at the same time, a new look for cigarette packaging. On the old green pack the Lucky Strike red circle, the target, appeared only on one side. Knowing that they sold in the millions, I decided to display the target on both sides so that the name Lucky Strike would be seen by twice as many people. I replaced the green with a shiny white and the pack looked more luminous; it was also cheaper to print, and the smell which the green ink had given off was gone.' Clearly, it would be necessary to get up very early in the morning to put one over on Mr Loewy.

Loewy's pack set off a whole series of imitators, the most distinguished of which is the French state tobacco monopoly Seita design for its Disque Bleu brand. A winged Viking helmet occupies the centre of a blue

circle in the centre of the soft paper pack. It was an early example of the continuing French fascination for all things transatlantic. And curiously, now that the old Disque Bleu pack has become synonymous with berets and 2CVs, it is just as picturesquely French. The brave new French have moved on to crushproof boxes and snappier Virginia tobacco style packs for their new wares. Can Cordon Bleu hold out against les MacDo much longer?

Somehow, for all Loewy's vanities – he was forever buttonholing politicians and being photographed with the famous – he managed to produce a design that gave Lucky Strike an authentic style of its own. Marlboro, on the other hand, through over-enthusiastic attempts to put across the same all-American message, and aggressive attempts to link itself with dangerous outdoor sporting activities, looks less like a part of cowboy country, and more the universal symbol of spivdom. It has become the favoured brand smoked by upwardly mobile wideboys from Lagos to Kiev. And this is appropriate, really, since its gung-ho American associations have always been questionable: the brand name was originally spelt with an 'ough' at the end, and came from England.

Coke bottles, cigarette packets and cigar boxes all come with at least some visible content. Perrier bottles on the other hand look empty even when they are full. Perrier might taste better than tap water, and is

often safer, but without the bottle it would be an unsaleable product in its largest markets. The Perrier boom is built around a product that is all about being both smart, and, in some not quite specified way, French. Both are properties that only work off French soil. The real French mineral water is Vichy, which with its stocky bottle and metallic taste is about as appealing as cod liver oil, and yet it embodies the essence of those endless all-night train journeys in long green SNCF trains, and zinc-countered brasseries. Perrier does come from France, Vergèze in the Gard to be precise, but it was the idea of an Englishman (St John Harmsworth, brother of the newspaper tycoon) to bottle it, and it was he who hit upon the distinctive tapering bottle, modelled on an Indian club seen out East.

All these non-Gallic origins haven't stopped Perrier's rapid rise in social acceptability over the past ten years. The green bottle, the elaborate Edwardian trademark, the fizzy and tasteless contents, have insinuated themselves so deeply into the psyche of the quiche-eating classes that they have become essential props.

There are those who would have you believe that the meaning of life, the secret of the universe, and the inner nature of mankind can all be determined from a close scrutiny of the contents of the average litter bin, sifting through the discarded wrappers, and empty bottles, and all the other débris of package-obsessed Western society. A few

particularly dedicated, and strong-stomached, enthusiasts, have dedicated their lives to this proposition. They have built up exhaustive collections of biscuit tins, and turned themselves into cataloguers of every type of tin, bottle and can ever produced.

It is true that there is a powerful magic about some packs. They have deliberately been designed to create a powerful sense of identity, and are reproduced in hundreds of millions. In the early days of packaging, in the most primitive phase, all that was required was high volume. That is to say, plenty of glitter and gold, swaggering lettering and bravado that all conspired to create a sense of magnificence. Over the years that has changed. There are certain types of product which it doesn't pay to package in covers that shout too loudly. Understatement spells quality better than boasting; the Benson and Hedges gold pack, for example, has gone from a premium product to market leader, and gloss black packs are now used to persuade smokers to pay over the odds. Is understatement now a form of bragging in itself? Certainly, packaging is not for amateurs any more, too much is at stake.

The modern world caught up with the pack in the 1940s and 1950s, streamlining, cleaning up, simplifying, with all the vigour that the Design Council could induce. All that has now gone into reverse, however, with the 1970s nostalgia boom. Ironically

enough, all the fake Victoriana that swamped packaging the second time around was intended to signify wholesome, 'traditional' values, not the fairground hucksterism of the originals. Nothing demonstrated the turn around in pack vocabulary more clearly than the way the brewers, who had done their best to dump everything to do with old-style beer in the 1970s, back-pedalled furiously when the Watneys Red Revolution turned into one of the great marketing disasters of all time. Less than a decade later, all traces of the new/old Watneys were obliterated in an epidemic of neo-Victorian labels, names, cans, mirrors and mahogany-effect Formica.

Genuine cult packs need to have stamina to rise above these frantic swings of the pendulum. They cannot avoid being affected by changing perceptions, however. The Newcastle Brown bottle, for example, was for long regarded as a primitive throwback from the palaeolithic era of brown ale and cloth caps, both in its sturdy, bullnecked shape and its picturesque label. Its survival seemed like the result of stubborn regional independence, not to say innate working class conservatism, too.

Newcastle Brown was the Staffordshire bull terrier of beers, a dusty throwback to a long-departed age before comprehensive schools and television had turned Britain into a homogeneous and homogenized paradise of shopping centres and fast food. According to the marketing people's logic,

the brand should have been killed off in the 1960s. But, somehow, it managed to cling to life long enough to turn itself from being a throwback into a fashionable product. The very qualities of strong individuality and distinctive flavour that once condemned it became assets.

As the fame of Newcastle Brown began to spread, it inevitably started to lose some of the 'authenticity' that it had once had. If all those smart London trendies wanted to be seen drinking the stuff, and what's more started to talk about it, it could hardly maintain its roots with its original audience. Eventually, the can replaced the bottle, and a cult object ended up being killed by its own success.

Something similar is happening to the Dutch beer, Grolsch. The sober Dutch evolved a beer, whose bottle has changed very little in shape since the turn of the century. It boasts a refastenable top, a tribute to much more temperate drinking habits than generally prevail in Britain. Apart from that wire-clip top, the Grolsch bottle is a triumph of the glassblower's art. The thick brown glass is patterned with fist-deep etched ornament. And yet this apparently timeless and down to earth example of packaging has now taken the British market by storm. So much so, indeed, that the Grolsch bottle is now in the process of acquiring ersatz competitors. Long lost bottlemaking techniques are being resurrected in an attempt by British

brewers to come up with an approximation to the heroically proportioned original.

By its very nature, packaging is an ephemeral business, in which images are consumed with indecent and greedy haste, and in which designers must struggle to provide an ever changing flow of new images. As the years have gone by, it has become a more and more sophisticated process. Highly trained teams of graduates research the nuances of every flourish, serif, and bold rule on a pack.

Even the professionals are now aware of the speed with which fashions change; they have seen their own work brought in to facelift tired old designs from the 1960s, discarded in favour of a retread of the very images they discarded, now given a fresh lease of period charm. This year's dull old cliché quickly becomes the year after next's nostalgia trip. Even gawkiness is now being designed in. Look at Stolichnaya Vodka, the genuine Comecon firewater, complete with uncalculatingly dumb label showing a factory, glued on slightly squint, and printed on low-grade paper. When the first Western vodkas started being marketed in the wake of the 007 boom, pack designs did their best to look glossy and sophisticated. Now they are all after the Stolichnaya artlessness because it looks authentic, and therefore suddenly takes on an air of sophistication. Small wonder that this is not a business for veterans. Packaging designers tend to burn out with the speed of commodity brokers.

Left: Grolsch's retention of the once common wire-clip stopper is a testament to the sober drinking habits of the Dutch. It adds a touch of exotic authenticity in its export markets

Chapter Seven

Transports of delight

Life after Lada land, and how to keep ahead of the Joneses. Selling the stately home on wheels. And is the car really the cathedral of the twentieth century

Some cars just don't belong. You could not, for example, expect to be able to drive a shiny new Datsun, or even a rusty old one for that matter, through the main gate at Buck House, park it on the gravel in the inner courtyard, and imagine you could get away with such a flagrant act of lese-majesty unscathed. The jauntiest of treads, and the most confident of smiles would falter beneath the withering contempt contained in the silent gaze of the legions of royal flunkies. Nothing would be said, of course. But even the thickest-skinned would get the message loud and clear that something was wrong. It would be almost as bad as attempting to wear brown shoes at a royal garden party.

This unfortunate aspect of the Datsun's image has nothing to do with the fact that it is a Japanese import – although that is a factor that has had the folks at Nissan worried enough to feel obliged, until very recently, to call their cars Datsuns for fear of having them too closely associated with the handy little tanks they used to make in the old days. Nor is it a matter of price. You can't help it if you can't afford a Bentley, but even distressed gentlefolk are expected to display a little elementary taste.

Compare the impression created by the Datsun, a dumb chrome-decked lump, with the Mini. The latter is a design that has been left substantially unchanged in all but the inessentials for twenty-five years. The former goes through model changes every year: they give it an American look one year, and a European flavour the next. Anyone can afford a Mini if they can afford a car at all. And yet ownership still bestows the reflected glory of one of the rare triumphs of British car design. Datsuns reflect nothing but the breezy, brash confidence of the brand. The Mini's success is subtler, a rare combination of engineering brilliance, astute image manipulation, and a design that blatantly panders to the driver's

ego. Ironically, the all-conquering Nissan were the people who once manufactured Austins under licence in Japan.

Back in the 1950s, fresh from his triumphant success with the Morris Minor, the Mini's creator Alec Issigonis saw the need for a car that, while it was small enough to weave around town in, still performed like a real car. To shave precious inches off its length, he mounted the engine transversely across the body, realizing for the first time that engines were perfectly happy to push a car in a different direction from that in which their valves were aligned. For its time the Mini was tiny, not much larger than the joke bubble cars still on the roads, with its ten-inch wheels. To overcome any such unflattering associations, the company was careful to dish out complimentary models to the taste-makers of the day who were soon to be seen dashing around town in them. Even Snowdon had one.

Still more important for its success, the Mini made up for its diminutive size by performing with almost indecent enthusiasm. Continentals who began by scoffing were quickly dazzled by its way of appearing from nowhere in their rear-view mirrors, nipping in and out of seemingly microscopic gaps in the autoroute traffic to overtake, and then disappearing once more over the horizon. This highly satisfactory image was reinforced by sports car detailing. There were rope door handles,

utilitarian sliding windows, and high tech welts over the bonnet. Even the ignition was a switch, located between the driver and his co-pilot. It made you feel exactly like a Spitfire ace, shooting it out with the Heinkels.

The Mini reinforced the truth that everyone has always known, that there is more to buying a car than simply acquiring a functional mode of transport. Cars have the ability to exude character and personality that is all their own. They have the capacity to suggest homely virtues, or exotic raffishness, vulgar ostentation or thoroughbred elegance. Back in the 1960s Michael Caine succinctly put it all into words when he told us that in England 'We think that Lancias are the kind of car that hairdressers drive.' Once that kind of image has been established it is almost impossible to break down. British Leyland, for example, desperately tried to portray the Jaguar (before they sold the whole company) as some kind of minor stately home on wheels, accompanied by the perceptible whiff of leather and cigar smoke, but the Sloanes have always known that there is something not quite right about it. Poor secondhand value has ensured that quite a few specimens have ended up in the wrong hands. What is more, four-door saloons with high performance engines lend themselves particularly well to the highly specialized and exacting requirements of the bank-robbing classes.

Left: In the early days, being at the controls of a Mini let loose on the unsuspecting autostradas of Europe was to feel like a Spitfire ace, trouncing the Heinkels

Below: Alec Issigonis's first triumph, the Mini's predecessor, was the Morris Minor, shown here in its half-timbered version, known as the Traveller. Now it's become the exclusive preserve of the social-working classes, a chariot of Fair Isle

There are those who will attempt to persuade you that all this kind of image building is a preoccupation of effete metropolitan sophisticates. Out in the sticks, where real men drink pints in straight glasses, the aforementioned real men drive about in Ladas, they will tell you. Despite the sneers of effete southerners, they are cheap, unpretentious cars, free of superfluous stylistic frills, or so goes the theory. Now while it is true that there are more Eastern European cars on the roads the further you get away from London, it is important to realize that far from opting out of the style stakes, their owners are making just as strong a personal statement with a Lada as any other owner. Sartorially, its equivalent is wearing black socks with open-toe sandals. Defiantly untrendy it may be, but neutral it is not.

One of the structuralist philosopher Roland Barthes' more questionable propositions was to suggest that you could put the production of a motor car in the same creative league as the building of a medieval cathedral. The idea was unconvincing in the 1950s when he first wrote about Citroën's basking shark limousine, the DS 19. Today, as a rapid tour around a modern car factory will convince anyone, it is utterly inappropriate. Market research was never part of a master mason's brief, nor was competition from Japan much of a worry. The major difficulty for the creative endeavour, or spiritually uplifting

view of things, is that there are so few people left on the shop floor. From the indoor railway siding at one end of the plant, where tightly coiled rolls of steel are brought in to be turned into car-shaped pieces by towering cutting presses, to the assembly lines where robots hunt in packs, there is not a soul to be seen. As the robots toil away uncomplainingly, darting and swooping over the entrails of half-finished cars, pausing from time to time to wipe the beads of sweat from their vision cameras, there is just the occasional passerby, a manager in a white coat with a clipboard, or a blue-overalled worker, cycling nonchalantly past, for all the world like a French farmer on his way through the country lanes.

The little human work that can be seen in progress hardly suggests the titanic cathedral building struggle with the elements or man attempting to impose his will on raw nature. Instead, there are silent acolytes, solicitously bending over robots that look as fragile as kitchen mixers. The vestigial production line workers struggle to keep pace with an ever flowing torrent of car bodies, stuffing in a cushion here, adding a piece of black rubber trim there.

In Barthes' terms, if there are any descendants of the cathedral builders left, then they are the craftsmen who model clay in the auto-styling studios, the designers armed with felt pens who sketch endless variations for the instrument panel and

bandy about fabric swatches, the engineers who tinker with the moving parts, and of course the accountants who see that it is all built to a price. Given the economies of scale of the car business, these individuals will very likely be in a different country, or even another continent from the plants that finally build their creations.

Cathedrals were the product of the direct involvement of the designer with the maker; and the dependence of one on the other blurred the distinctions between them. Modern car-building, on the other hand, relies on a production line stripped of even the most basic skills. Accordingly, the barriers between designer and maker have been sharpened to an unprecedented degree. Those cutting presses, for example, look like giant automatic sandwich vending machines because they have been equipped with neon-lit windows to show passersby what is going on. It seems suspiciously like a condescending gesture, one which turns the workforce into mere spectators.

It is precisely because of all this dehumanization and rigid control that cars are, of all artefacts, those most likely to become cult objects. Such are the standards of mechanical perfection to which they can aspire that cars are the most powerful and universally recognized of cults. Volkswagen were quite truthfully able to portray the Beetle side by side with a Coke bottle in one of their ads as the larger one of 'two shapes known the world over'.

Every single part of a car, from the door handles to the headlamps, from the engine to the transmission, has been pored over by a team of experts. Setting up a production line is so expensive that there is no room for mistakes. Models are made, prototypes built, market researchers consulted and production techniques optimized. Of course the result of all this is just as likely to be cautious uniformity as it is to be perfection. In the case of just a few models, however, all these elements come together in a way that amounts to far more than the sum of their parts. These are the cars that have a presence that is as strong as any ikon. Subtly they imply that they are no mere manmade object, but are instead some kind of ideal form.

The car-makers have long recognized that they have to cater for the stylistic sensibilities of their customers if they are to survive. Even in the golden age of Detroit tin, when Oldsmobile vied with Chevrolet in the rush to scrape the heavens with their tail fins, their ads promised, 'You aren't just buying a car, with us you are buying an image.'

The problem for so many manufacturers has been that they can't deliver the promise. Just exactly what kind of image is a Datsun Laurel or a Honda Civic projecting? Even their owners have difficulty finding them in carparks, and it is this failing that explains the presence of at least one silent, but attentive, Japanese tyro in almost every

design studio of note in the world, quietly listening and learning.

The most successful cult car of all must surely be the Volkswagen Beetle, designed by Ferdinand Porsche, still in production over fifty years after its inception, of which 20 million cars have come off the lines. It may have been banished from its native Germany to factories in Brazil and Mexico, but those Third-World models are still in buoyant demand in Europe, and there they can command a premium price, which is more than can be said for the outmoded Fiats now being built under licence in Eastern Europe. Even in sheer numbers, the Beetle runs the Japanese close to claiming the highest figures for any car ever built.

Ferdinand Porsche, an electrical engineer turned car designer, with such exotic models as the Mercedes SS sportscar to his credit, had long nurtured an ambition to build a people's car, an updated Model T Ford for Europe. It was to be a practical, utilitarian model, making use of the latest techniques and advanced engineering to bring motoring to the German masses. It was an unlikely combination of Adolf Hitler and the British Army who allowed him to realize his dream.

Hitler paid for the Volkswagen's development in the 1930s, when he had the worrisome habit of calling it the 'strength through joy car', or KdfWagen. The prototypes were no sooner ready at the VW plant, built naturally in a completely new town named the Stadt der KdfWagens in 1938, than war broke out, and the production lines were turned over to building VW-based jeeps and cooking stoves for the Russian front. British army engineers rescued the place from chaos after the war and got the factory producing Volkswagens in commercial quantities for the first time, presumably as a therapeutic alternative to playing cricket and football with the locals. While they were about it, they renamed the town, Wolfsburg – so much snappier in the long run.

Porsche's most unquestioning admirers would have you believe that he designed the Volkswagen in exactly the same way that the Bauhaus architects built their buildings: that he started by pretending that nobody had ever built a car before, so that there were to be no precedents for how it should look, but instead considered every part of the car from first principles. Certainly, like the Bauhaus architects, he did have a little trouble keeping the rain out of the engine, but the design did owe a little to the Detroit of the 1930s, and quite a lot to the little known Czech car, the Tatra V8 of 1937.

Both the Beetle and the Tatra had a bulbous body to provide the maximum stability, allowing the VW to dispense with a separate girder frame structure. Even more radically, Porsche put the VW's engine at the back of the car, to the abiding confusion of those who open the bonnet

Left: The details have all changed, what was once a narrow slit has widened into a proper rear window, and the bulbous curves of the last European production model verged on self-parody, but the Beetle is still recognizably Dr Porsche's creation

looking for a dipstick and find nothing but a luggage rack. The idea was to concentrate weight over the back axle, and to cut down on the drive shaft. An air-cooled engine overcame the risk from conventional water-cooled radiators which tended to boil in summer and freeze in winter.

When the British took over Wolfsburg, they had the place going well enough to build 6000 VWs in 1947. Heinz Nordhoff, an ex-GM man, who had done time in Detroit, was installed as the civilian manager in the following year, and he was quickly able to treble production, eventually building 1.6 million cars a year by 1968. The British military genius for improvisation kept the factory going on bartered raw materials in the early days. But when army engineers, justifiably proud of their achievements, attempted to hand the concern over to a British or American car manufacturer to run commercially, they got short shrift. The Beetle, it seemed, was too bizarre to be taken seriously.

Lord Rootes headed an Allied commission sent out to Germany to investigate the plant in 1946, and was unimpressed. 'A car like this,' he wrote, 'will remain popular for two or three years, if that. To build the car commercially would be a completely uneconomic enterprise.' The American representative was even less enthusiastic. 'Mr Ford,' reported Ernest Breech to his master in Dearborn, 'I don't think that what we are being offered here is worth a damn.'

The rest, of course, is history.

It is worth remembering that the VW wasn't a cult right from the start, and did not achieve cult status until it was boosted in America by some particularly clever and subtle advertising. Doyle Dane and Bernbach took over the VW account in 1959, and they deliberately decided to play up the Beetle's quirky cussedness against the flash chrome of its homegrown competitors. While Detroit added more and more cosmetic variations to its models every year, VW made a point of the fact that it stayed the same. It was a tactic that quickly made it the smart, Eastern establishment car to drive, a protest against built-in obsolescence and superfluous gimmickry. Actually the VW did change over the years, getting ever more bulbous and bug-like until it eventually became a parody of itself. And in the process it became ever more of a cult object, culminating in the Beetleiest Beetle of them all, the 1970s black open-top version.

The bug evolved slowly. In its palaeolithic phase it had a tiny slit of a rear window, with a strut dividing it in two for stability's sake. The strut disappeared in 1952. And a year later the previously plain front window acquired a quarter light. In 1955 flashing lights replaced odd little orange flipper arms as directional indicators. In 1956 the rear window became a neat oval, and the car sprouted businesslike chromed twin exhausts. In 1958 VW went to Turin to have the rear window enlarged. In 1960 the

Left: The Führer's people's car on parade. The British Army got the Strength through Joy car, as Hitler called it, into production for the first time, but couldn't interest Ford or Rootes in taking it on

Below: Still going strong after nearly 50 years, on production lines in Mexico and Brazil, the Beetle is the most successful car of all time when measured in sheer numbers

bonnet badge was restyled; Wolfsburg's coat of arms took on a less heraldic look, and in 1962 bigger tail lights appeared, starting off a process that was to continue until the Beetle finally fossilized on the Latin American production lines in 1978. Even then the Beetle was still fundamentally a product of the Emil and the Detectives era of 1930s Europe, apparently almost naïvely simple in its looks, but in fact finely calculated.

The other great survivor of the car industry is the product of thinking very close to that of the VW, and was born at roughly the same time: work on the Citroën 2CV began in 1936. Pierre Boulanger, Citroën's chief designer, who was also responsible for much of the inspiration behind the other two Citroën cult cars, the Traction Avant of 1934 and the DS 19 of the 1950s, set out with the 2CV to create a car that would be cheap, rugged and economical. It was to be a car that a French farmer could use to take his vegetables to market across mud tracks. It didn't have to go very fast, but it had to be roomy, economical to run, and above all extremely cheap. Like Porsche, Boulanger went back to first principles. 'I want an umbrella on four wheels,' he told his staff. The first 250 2CVs were built before 1939, with such an emphasis on economy that they had just one headlamp, and only a single windscreen wiper. Rather than go in for complicated winding mechanisms that would take the

windows down into the door panels, the car had simple folding glass flaps. All but one of that first batch were destroyed to keep them out of the hands of the Germans; the sole survivor, carefully hidden, emerged after the Second World War to form the basis of France's modern car industry.

Outside France the 2CV is seen as the embodiment of Gallic charm, as French as Disque Bleu and Beaujolais. It is the ideal car for the herbivorous polytechnic lecturer who is not quite ready for the robustly functional Renault 4 van. It implies a refusal to take car ownership entirely seriously, a feeling that it is not a heavyweight consumer possession, but almost as benign a piece of technology as the bicycle.

On its home ground in France, the 2CV is seen rather differently. The French detest the view that the outside world has of them as bucolics in blue overalls with baguettes clutched under their arms. They want to be seen to be sophisticated and technologically advanced. Strictly speaking, the 2CV with its air-cooled engine, and pressed metal body could be described as exactly that. But, to French eyes, it now simply spells low-budget utility. And the French much prefer the toothy star blaster looks of the DS 19 line that culminated in the most shark-like Citroën of them all, the Citroën Maserati, which not only went indecently fast, but came with grinning chrome teeth too. The same look extends today even to the smaller Citroëns, the little Visas, with

Left: An umbrella on wheels, as its creator put it, the Deux Chevaux was designed to be just strong enough to get the French peasant and his produce to market, _and_ to come within his budget. Cutting the costs to that price meant omitting such non-essentials as a second headlamp

Below: In nearly 50 years, Citroën haven't been able to come up with an equal in popularity and charm to the basic 2CV original. Essentially it's a Gallic alternative to the Beetle, having been planned at around the same time

nattily styled high tech controls.

Ironically, if there is a car in France that fills the role of the 2CV in England, it is the Mini. At just about the time when the Mini's charms began to pall in Britain, at the start of the 1970s, it became *Le* car for the stylish young Parisian about town.

The trouble with all cars, however, is that they offer surprisingly little scope for showing off in. You can't casually ask your friends over to admire your new car in the same way that you can ask them over for a drink so that they can't help noticing your gleaming new chrome and black leather sofa, or your bookshelves stocked with tidy orange-spined Penguin paperbacks. Every now and again you can offer people a lift, but the chances are that they will leave muddy footprints on the carpet and make nervous clucking noises as you overtake on the inside lane. All you can do is to arrange to be seen getting in and out of the thing in

Right: The most outrageous motorized phallic object ever produced is not the E-Type – that dubious honour must go to Pontiac. But Jaguar made a pretty good attempt, managing at the same time to introduce a touch of well-bred English sportiness that established the car as a model for every fast car designer since

the right sort of locations – seldom a dignified process – or else flash gracefully by, waving casually. All this means that people need to be highly tuned to the nuances of car-speak to get the point at all. And that is why manufacturers resort to such strenuous image-building campaigns. Why else after all would Jaguar go to all the trouble of paying handsomely to have their cars beaten into eighth place on the Le Mans circuit? This need to impress on

the run explains the emphasis and attention given to names, numbers and logos on the back of the car. At least your fellow drivers will have something to read as you idle away the time in a jam. And it also explains why so much of the styling effort is directed toward making the driver of the car feel better.

It is possible to style up virtually any motoring virtue, even those of safety or utility, in a way that will give drivers a

Right: Star of countless Swinging London movies, the Minimoke was a low budget Mini spin-off. A '60s icon that somehow manages to encapsulate the novelty-obsessed Harold Wilson years

warm glow inside. Witness the emphasis that manufacturers like Mercedes and Volvo put on how safe their products are. Boxy, tank-like looks conspire to suggest that anything you happen to come across around a sharp bend had better get out of the way, or else they are going to bounce off your dodgem-car-sized bumpers. Volvo take things to their logical conclusion, ushering in the age of welfare state motoring in which nobody is allowed to hurt themselves without official permission. They build flashers and buzzers that nag unremittingly until you behave yourself and do up your seat belt. Even then the car keeps its headlamps on permanently: Auntie Volvo knows best, dear. How long will it be before the car refuses to start until its sensors detect that you have extinguished your cigarette? The Volvo stationwagon is the consumerist car par excellence. It's large enough in the back to take a week's shopping

Right: The Volvo is not just a sturdy and sensible car under the bonnet, it has been styled up to look safe too, with its intimidating bumpers and impossible to turn off headlamps. Not so much a motor car, more a way of life

and a couple of smelly Labradors, yet its image is so wholesome that there is no need for any troublesome guilt about conspicuous consumption. The mystery about the marque is to fathom whatever possessed its managers to style their most recent models on the lines of an American compact. It is rather like a dowager suddenly kicking over the traces and taking to rouge and slit skirts. The idea of making a style out of utility goes back as far as those cyclopean cloth-topped prewar Citroën 2CVs. The most recent incarnation is Fiat's Panda, which makes a lot of fuss about its utilitarian and 'economical' flat glass windscreen. The savings, for a mass-produced car, of substituting flat glass for more overtly stylish curved windscreens are negligible, but it does help massage the driver's ego.

Interestingly, the utility look is now associated more and more with the toy cars, those models in which maximizing play value

Right: Giugiaro saw his design for Fiat's Panda as an update of the old Citroën 2CV: it was meant to look cheap and cheerful, hence the flat glass windscreen. But it was also the first car to have its seats designed to look like Habitat furniture

for adults is most of the point. The Jeep has spawned a whole tribe of more or less rugged descendants which fill this role. At one end is the faithful and dependable Land Rover: in performance terms it is the real thing, an off-road vehicle that will stand up to extremes. It has the same kind of appeal as the Barbour; its image as a sturdy workhorse intact, despite the attentions of those whose requirements attempt in vain to tax its surefootedness. Whether that wholesome image will survive the latest restyle is open to doubt. Leyland have been rash enough to deck its lights back and front with wire cages that spell, unmistakably, riot police. And it is worth remembering that, in certain parts of the world, revolutionary odes have been composed in praise of the Land Rover's liberating capacities.

At the other extreme is the Mini-Moke, which is the Mini stripped down for play

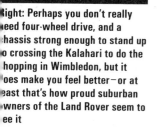

Right: Perhaps you don't really need four-wheel drive, and a chassis strong enough to stand up to crossing the Kalahari to do the shopping in Wimbledon, but it does make you feel better—or at least that's how proud suburban owners of the Land Rover seem to see it

with a canvas top, and no body to speak of. It was the star of countless Sixties frugging movies, in which our heroes sped across beaches waving cheerfully at head-scratching yokels on route. Suzuki scored something of a landmark by producing the first Japanese cult car with their diminutive miniaturized Range Rover copy that follows in the Moke's tyre marks.

In the old days chrome and fins sold cars. Now customers, jaded by a constant diet of glitter, require less obvious decorative flourishes to get their juices flowing. It was Volkswagen who first produced an alternative aesthetic with the Beetle, and took it even further with the spectacularly successful Golf, designed by Giorgetto Giugiaro, the international hired gunslinger of car design. He gave the Golf its dapper folded paper geometry, and stripped off almost all the chrome trim that had become an obligatory part of car styling. With a

Right: When Land Rover decided to restyle the basic model, they ran the risk of losing its image as an honest to goodness utilitarian workhorse. And, sure enough, they have. Instead of classic British engineering understatement, they opted for American style go-faster stripes

stroke of genius he gave the black and silver versions of the car a thin red line around the radiator grille: it was a touch that had suggestions of military design, something like the red dot on the black barrel of a Beretta Parabellum automatic, which shows the safety catch is off.

The Golf became an instant cult, in Britain as much of an essential Sloane Ranger accessory as Gucci loafers. And the style was set for a range of downmarket imitators, in particular the hotted-up Ford Escort models, in which suit jackets hang from rear windows. For Volkswagen, in serious economic difficulties at the end of the 1960s with a rapidly ageing and stunted product range, the success of the Golf came not a moment too soon. Without it the company could have faced oblivion.

The Golf was one of the last of the single designer cars, produced not by an international team in the manner of the

Right: By becoming <u>the</u> car for Europe's upwardly aspirational classes, the Golf, virtually singlehanded, rescued Volkswagen from the oblivion threatened by its inability to come up with anything else half as good as the Beetle

Sierra, but by an individual who left his particular stamp on it. But when the time for a Golf replacement came, the day of the name designer had passed, certainly as far as VW was concerned anyway. Giugiaro wasn't asked back to have another attempt at his creation. Instead, a studio full of technicians were allowed to have their way with it. The origami neatness of the original was bloated with middle-aged spread, and instead of being out on its own, the new

Golf became just one of the crowd.

Sex is popularly held to play a large role in the language of car design. It's certainly true that such classic cult objects as the E-type Jaguar do have a less than subtle phallic look. And other key models, such as the Renault Alpine, the Lamborghini Contach, and the Ferrari, demand of their passengers the agility of a limbo dancer. But none of these are true cult objects. They may inspire the mass-produced models

Right: Volkswagen fell out with Giugiaro over the restyling of the successor to the original Golf. They replaced his folded paper geometry with flabby curves that look just like middle-aged spread; sleek perhaps, but hardly a cult

that are the essential cults, but there are too many rough edges about these thoroughbreds for them to be as seamless and poised as a real cult object. And these days building a car by hand is so expensive that there is not enough left over for making instruments specially, so even in the most exotic models, these will often be bought off the peg, and give a component hifi non-matching look to the dashboard. The switches and knobs will suffer from the same problem – though, ironically, some genuine mass-produced models will adopt the same look to provide that customized flavour.

The Airstream trailer can be traced back to 1928, when something called the *Road Yacht* was first produced in an increasingly mobile America. It was a Dust Bowl version of the gipsy caravan, a trailer to be towed behind a car, not a horse, and equipped with a galley kitchen, toilet, storage space, and

Right: Sleek bullet-shaped aluminium brought streamlining to the masses in the 1930s. Named after the less than successful Chrysler Airflow, the Airstream trailer is still alive and well

enough room to sleep five, at a pinch. Such a product was naturally a prime candidate for the wave of streamlining mania that swept the world in the 1930s. The petrol gauge of the car doing the towing could demonstrate clearly the obvious benefits of presenting as little wind resistance as possible. Accordingly, a restyled bulbous metal bug on wheels, known as the *Airstream Clipper* was launched in 1936. Its descendants are still to be seen, not so much on the freeways, but on the two-lane blacktops of America, as quintessentially American as diners and Greyhound buses, and like them doomed to obscurity in the affluent all-plastic present that shuns such resolutely simple blue-collar pleasures.

The name and shape of the original Airstream seems to have been an attempt to cash in on the notoriety of the Chrysler Airflow of 1934, which, though a commercial flop on a scale not repeated until the Ford

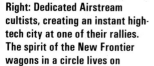

Right: Dedicated Airstream cultists, creating an instant high-tech city at one of their rallies. The spirit of the New Frontier wagons in a circle lives on

148

Edsel of the postwar years, achieved huge fame as the first truly streamlined American production car. With its bright aluminium finish, its radiused windows, and the suggestive way in which external bulges and bumps clearly express functions such as air-conditioning and heating, the Airstream has become a high tech ikon. Despite its downmarket associations, the styling is pure Buck Rogers-Star Wars-Futurism. The most memorable image of the Airstream is the sight of an enthusiasts convention, in which an instant city is created by gathering them in circles, pioneer-on-the-prairie style.

The now sadly defunct Checker cab is a similar piece of authentic and utterly unselfconscious Americana. Produced by the Checker Corporation on a modest production line until the start of the 1980s, the Checker was designed to stand up to the potholes that characterize the usual road surface in most American cities. Most companies operating them painted their fleets yellow, but in one or two outposts, such as Washington, other colour permutations can be seen. The Checker is the stately shire horse of car design, heavy and ponderous, but with its trim curves, nevertheless both handsome and dependable, its lines frozen in the Detroit of the 1950s. It is not, however, nearly so spacious as the world's only other purpose-built taxi, the British Austin-based FX 4 made by Carbodies of Coventry.

The British black taxi seats five in comfort, thanks to the two jump seats, and the division with the driving compartment is achieved with far more dignity than in American cabs. With its black leather seats, and well-ordered passenger compartment, its distinctive and discreet purring diesel engine, the British taxi is a gentleman's club on wheels. Long admired by smart Italian car designers such as Giugiaro, its days now seem to be numbered with the planned introduction of a Range Rover-based alternative. The taxi has, nevertheless, inspired a whole new class of vehicles: high-profile crosses between cars and vans, now being built by the Japanese and the French.

Another example of the very worthiness and reliability of a public service vehicle causing it to turn into a cult object is the classic London Routemaster bus. Even though it's been exported to such former colonies as Jamaica, India and Ghana, the stately, and surprisingly spritely, double-decker is known around the world as being as much an essential part of London's character as Big Ben and bobbies' helmets. There are today whole flocks of pretenders to the bus's mantle cruising the streets of London, for London Transport has been trying to come up with a more modern replacement ever since 1966. But all have been found wanting. Nothing has managed to equal the reliability, comfort and practicality of the original 1954 Routemaster, designed especially for

Left: Like the Checker cab in the United States, the London taxi looks doomed to extinction. The charm of this padded leather slice of clubland is to be replaced by a Range Rover spin-off

London Transport's use by designer Douglas Scott and engineer Eric Ottoway.

Between them, Scott and Ottoway produced a bus that not only looks so effortlessly right that it has become a design classic even while being so universally well known that it is virtually invisible, but one which also performs tirelessly in some of the most difficult operating conditions for any bus service in the world. London Transport's routes combine both leafy suburbs in which traffic moves quickly and heavily congested areas. The Routemaster takes them all in its stride, while lesser breeds go into the garage for constant repairs. The only thing that may one day doom the Routemaster to the scrapheap is London Transport's determination to weed its staff numbers down. The long-term plan is to turn its present two-man crews into driver only operations, and without a conductor to give a signal to the driver when it is safe to move off, the Routemaster becomes unusable.

From its teak floors to its specially patterned seat covers, the Routemaster was designed to be both hardwearing and comfortable. It offers the special thrills of an open-air rear platform, giving Londoners with sufficient agility the chance to live dangerously, leaping on and off at will – surely one of life's essential democratic freedoms – rather than be subject to the totalitarian whims of the much more authoritarian driver-controlled door.

For a vehicle designed in the 1950s, the Routemaster is remarkably miserly in its consumption of fuel. Scott and Ottoway were farsighted enough in their approach to juggle with the composition of such details as the seat upholstery, saving every last half ounce of horsehair stuffing that they could to keep the overall weight of the bus down to an astonishingly trim seven tons – a weight that compares extremely favourably with the ten-ton monsters common on Britain's roads today.

Scott and Ottoway put the engine and the driver's cab into the overall outline of the bus, a solution that not only looks neat, but which also gives the driver a good view high up over the traffic. Passengers are treated to such sensible and user-friendly features as winding windows in both the upper and lower saloons – to use London Transport's own telling description of the passenger compartments of this dignified conveyance. Seats were bolted securely to the bus walls to provide a firm, comfortable ride free of judders and jolts. One original detail that is now sadly disappearing is the bell cord that allows passengers to signal to the driver to stop.

The distinctive shade of scarlet used for the exterior paintwork has been a feature of London Transport vehicles ever since it was first formed from the welter of competing omnibus companies that once plied the streets of the capital. The original gold lettering, with the L in London, and the last T in transport larger than the rest has now been superseded by a less distinctive rendering of the LT bar across a circle logo that has become shorthand for mass transit all around the world.

No other bus, with the possible exception of Raymond Loewy's streamlined 1940s Greyhound comes anywhere near matching the Routemaster's charms.

The bicycle community is still a claustrophobic, closed world, dominated by the enthusiast and the buff, obsessed with the serious business of Reynolds hand-welded tubing, and Italian gears. It is peopled by the grimly earnest, who take a dour view of the frivolous newcomers who view cycling as a pleasure, and who treat cycles with less than religious devotion. It is noticeable, however, that certain key cycles have begun to crop up outside this world. The Motobecane 10 speed spells Yuppie in unmistakable terms, especially when it is deployed inside cramped but chic American apartments, preferably strung up in the hall on pulleys. The buffs resent this kind of behaviour with a special ferocity, for by treating the essence of their obsessions, lightweight high-performance machines, as decorative frills, the whole basis of the cult is being undermined. And yet that is what is happening. It is no use having any old bike cluttering up your pad if you want the kudos that comes with it. In England the position is slightly different. Huge old boneshakers equipped with

baskets and no brakes are perfectly acceptable in certain circles.

The real cult bicycle is undoubtedly the Moulton, designed by Dr Alex Moulton, one of those boffin figures that continually figure prominently in British life. The engineering efficiency of the small-wheeled shock absorber equipped Moulton will always be a subject of heated contention. Some claim the tiny wheels make it dangerously unstable. Others maintain exactly the opposite. But it did come along at a time when the world was going Mini-crazy after the hemline, and the car designed by Moulton's friend, Alec Issigonis.

Twenty years later, Moulton tried to repeat the success of the first Moulton, with a high tech version for the 1980s. It offered the performance of a ten-speed racing version, yet with the same small wheels of the original. Its cost, and the unique open-mesh girder structure seem set to make it into another cult. The original Moulton dragged cycling into the swinging Sixties, rescuing it from the cloth cap and whippet image that lingered on into the 1970s, with its advocates of oatmeal and ecology, who took to cycling in a big way.

Right: An example of a cult that didn't last. Briefly in the '60s the world went mad for minis, and that included Dr Alex Moulton's diminutively wheeled bicycle

Chapter Eight

Pride of possessions

The difference between matt black professionalism and pale pastel playfulness; and why bright yellow is taking over from both

That possessions should have a symbolic as well as a functional role is nothing new. They have always been used by their owners to put across their wealth, position and taste. Once, when status was measured by individually produced possessions, it was the quality of the workmanship, and the preciousness of the materials with which they were made, that counted. Now, when we make do with mass-produced products, available in an abundance that would have been inconceivable in any other era, rather different qualities have become important.

Mass-produced products still have the capacity to take on their own distinct identities and personality, and it is their command of these attributes that gives them such charm as they may, or may not, possess. The rules have changed, however. Now that we all own so much more than our grandparents did, it is no longer the fact that we possess a car or a colour television set that is important, it is the *brand* that people notice.

Cult Objects are a product of this production-line era, and are an entirely modern phenomenon. Design has taken the place that craft used to hold in determining the character of our possessions. And cult objects are designed and manufactured to perfection. Sometimes it is still an unconscious process, but more often, in a period in which the visual language of design has become so widely disseminated, it is a highly self-conscious and deliberate business.

The elements of design language can sometimes, when deployed with sufficient skill, be used to fabricate a cult object. Or, alternatively, and more frequently, they can be used to decode the message that a cult object which is already in existence is putting across. Thus, black metal finishes are almost universally used to signify 'serious' and 'professional'. Pastel shades are for toys – or for products that want to hint that they might be as much for pleasure as for business. Yellow has become the code for underwater gear; applied now to cameras, binoculars and even personal cassette players. The unstated but implied message is that anything that a diver is going to use 20 fathoms down is not only tough and sporty, but glamorous too. Olive drab and stencil serial number logos are all about militaria – with all the attendant macho, rugged implications. Epaulettes project the same kind of image. Elaborate but discreet packaging signifies quality. So-called sports clothes – primary colours, stripes, boldly emblazoned with the name of their manufacturer – project health and fitness – and so on.

As with all languages, meanings change, or become subtly modified with time. Some 'words' become archaic, and drop out of use altogether – chrome, perhaps, is one example. Others through overuse become worn out clichés, and are best avoided. The fact that design has turned into such a widely used language, and one which is so universally exposed, has increased these pressures. Design is the means by which manufacturers differentiate one essentially identical product from another, and is thus quite literally consumed.

By definition this kind of design cannot last, and its purveyors are constantly scouring the world for fresh sources of visual invention. Change is the essential ingredient in the image-building process, when it is being used to stimulate demand. How, after all, can one product be made to look fresh, appealing and interesting, unless another is at the same time declining into datedness. But there is no need to get too worried about this apparently profligate use of imagery. What Vance Packard failed to take into account in *The Waste Makers*, his primly puritanical attack on the golden age of Detroit tin, was that looking dated is only the first step on the now extremely short journey to period charm, nostalgia and finally classic status. Once the process took decades. Victoriana was mocked right up until the late 1960s. Now, such is our hunger for new sources of imagery, that the worst excesses of 1970s style – platform heels and Heavy Metal – are already taking on a certain period charm. Nothing is wasted now, not even built-in visual obsolescence. Of course, raking over a style for the second or third time – most period styles nowadays tend to contain revivalist elements of a previous look – sharpens up our sensitivity to visual nuances no end. At one level this allows us to adopt a certain irony and distance: 'No, it's OK, I know this is bad taste, and I don't really mean it' is the first message of a revival. 'Look at this period classic' is the second, and so on.

At another and more significant level, it enormously increases the subtlety and range of uses to which the language of design can be put. The more we all get accustomed to the visual clues used by various styles, the

Right: The sculptor Bertoia was asked by Knoll to produce a piece of furniture in the 1950s. It is still in production, moving, ironically, from up-to-the-minute modernity to tongue-in-cheek period piece in the intervening years

more that can be done with less.

Image-building advertising relies heavily on this process. Television and glossy magazine commercials in particular are key methods both for the dissemination of the message conveyed by particular objects, and as the media by which that message is consumed. One often-used technique is known as design propping. In essence this means leaving a suggestive-looking cult object somewhere in view on the set, or in the picture. A Le Corbusier chair perhaps, or possibly a Tizio light. At first the message that is put across is that your product, be it a brand of recording tape, or a variety of personal computer, is just as much a reflection of its owner's taste and distinction as the cult object whose company it is seen to be keeping. But at another level such advertisements also put out a message about the cult objects themselves – that they are in some way special or interesting, or why

Right: Nick Butler designed a torch for the battery manufacturer Duracell with the express purpose of selling more of their products. By turning it into a matt black high-tech fantasy that maximizes the tactile qualities of the switch and the mechanism, he has done just that